MORE TRUE STORIES

SECOND EDITION

A HIGH-BEGINNING READER

by Sandra Heyer

INTRODUCTION

MORE TRUE STORIES is a high-beginning reader for students of English as a Second Language. It consists of 22 units based on human-interest stories adapted from newspapers and magazines. The vocabulary and structures used in the stories are carefully controlled to match those of a typical beginning ESL class. At the same time, all attempts were made to keep the language natural.

In answer to those students who think some stories are too amazing to be true: Yes, the stories are true, to the best of our knowledge. A special "To the Teacher" section at the back of the book provides additional information about each story.

Following are some suggestions for using MORE TRUE STORIES. Teachers new to the field might find these suggestions especially helpful. Please remember that these are only suggestions. Teachers should, of course, feel free to adapt these strategies to best suit their teaching styles and their students' learning styles.

PRE-READING

Beneath the photo that introduces each unit are two sets of questions. The first set guides students as they describe the photo. The second set asks students to speculate on the content of the reading.

If the pre-reading activity is done orally in class, you might prompt students to describe the photo by saying, "Look at the picture. What do you see?" Sometimes students respond more readily to the question "What do you see?" than to a more specific question (i.e., "Who are these people?"). When asked a specific question, some students are reluctant to speak; they assume there is a specific correct answer. When asked "What do you see?" they are more inclined to respond because it is clearer that any reasonable answer is acceptable.

If your students are comfortable speaking English, you may wish to guide them into posing their own pre-reading questions. After the class describes the photo and reads the title of the story, ask, "What do you want to know?" Write the students' questions on the board. Return to the questions after reading the story to see which were answered.

READING THE STORY

If your students understand spoken English well but have little experience reading, you may wish to begin by reading the story aloud, or by playing the tape recording of the story. If the story has a surprise ending, you could pique students' interest by stopping short of the last few paragraphs. Students who have a tendency to stop at every unknown word should be encouraged to read the story twice, once without stopping to get the gist of the story, and then a second time, stopping to underline new vocabulary.

THE EXERCISES

Each unit has four types of exercises: vocabulary, comprehension, discussion, and writing. Students can complete the exercises individually, in pairs, in small groups, or with the whole class. The exercises can be completed in class or assigned as homework. At the back of the book there is an answer key to the exercises.

Vocabulary. The vocabulary exercises highlight words that ESL students identified as new and that could be clearly drawn, described, or defined. The exercises clarify meaning while giving students practice in establishing meaning through contextual clues.

Comprehension. The comprehension exercises test students' understanding of the story; more important, the exercises help students develop reading skills they will use throughout their reading careers—skills such as scanning, summarizing, identifying the main idea, and recognizing connectors and other rhetorical devices.

Discussion. Most of the discussion exercises require students to complete a task—to fill in a chart, to interview a classmate, to draw a picture or a map—so that there is a concrete focus to the discussion. The task-centered exercises make it possible for students to talk without the direct supervision of the teacher, a necessity in large classes.

Several of the discussion exercises ask students to share information about their native countries with a partner from a different country. Teachers whose students are learning English in their native countries will need to modify those exercises that are designed for the multinational classroom.

Writing. Most of the writing exercises are structured. Students rewrite a story in the past tense, create a list, complete a story, or write a paragraph on a specific topic. Students who are fairly accomplished writers may need a more challenging assignment, such as writing a short essay. Students who are less experienced writers may need to see some samples before they write.

The vocabulary, comprehension, discussion, and writing exercises are at approximately parallel levels; that is, they assume that students speak and write about as well as they read. Of course, that is not always the case. Please feel free to tamper with the exercises—to adjust them up or down to suit students' proficiency levels, to skip some, or to add some of your own.

Both the exercises and reading selections are intended to build students' confidence along with their reading skills. Above all, it is hoped that reading MORE TRUE STORIES will be a pleasure, for both you and your students.

CONTENTS

UNIT 1

1. PRE-READING

Look at the picture.

- What is the dog doing?

Read the title of the story. Look at the picture again.

- Where do you think the dog is going?
- What do you think this story is about?
- Can you guess what happens?

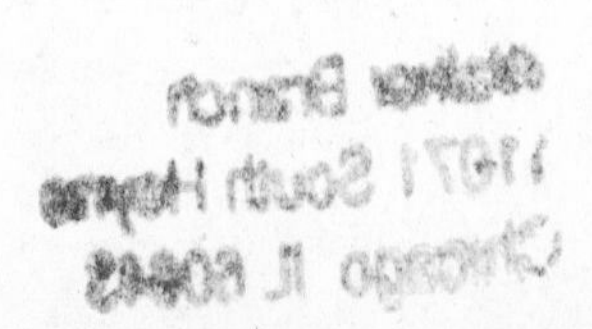

Puppy Love

"Shiro! Shiro!"

Mr. and Mrs. Nakamura were worried. Their dog Shiro was missing. "Shiro!" they called again and again. Mr. and Mrs. Nakamura lived on a small island in Japan. They looked everywhere on the island, but they couldn't find Shiro.

The next day Mr. Nakamura heard a noise at the front door. He opened the door, and there was Shiro. Shiro was very wet, and he was shivering.

A few days later Shiro disappeared again. He disappeared in the morning, and he came back late at night. When he came back, he was wet and shivering.

Shiro began to disappear often. He always disappeared in the morning and came back late at night. He was always wet when he came back.

Mr. Nakamura was curious. "Where does Shiro go?" he wondered. "Why is he wet when he comes back?"

One morning Mr. Nakamura followed Shiro. Shiro walked to the beach, ran into the water, and began to swim. Mr. Nakamura jumped into his boat and followed his dog. Shiro swam for about two miles.[1] Then he was tired, so he climbed onto a rock and rested. A few minutes later he jumped back into the water and continued swimming.

Shiro swam for three hours. Then he arrived at an island. He walked onto the beach, shook the water off, and walked toward town. Mr. Nakamura followed him. Shiro walked to a house. A dog was waiting in front of the house. Shiro ran to the dog, and the two dogs began to play. The dog's name was Marilyn. Marilyn was Shiro's girlfriend.

Marilyn lived on Zamami, another Japanese island. Shiro and the Nakamuras used to live on Zamami. Then the Nakamuras moved to Aka, a smaller island. They took Shiro with them. Shiro missed Marilyn very much and wanted to be with her. But he wanted to be with the Nakamuras, too. So, Shiro lived with the Nakamuras on the island of Aka and swam to Zamami to visit Marilyn.

People were amazed when they heard about Shiro. The distance from Aka to Zamami is two and a half miles,[2] and the ocean between the islands is very rough. "Nobody can swim from Aka to Zamami!" the people said.

Shiro became famous. Many people went to Zamami because they wanted to see Shiro. During one Japanese holiday, 3,000 people visited Zamami. They waited on the beach for Shiro. "Maybe Shiro will swim to Zamami today," they said. They all wanted to see Shiro, the dog who was in love.

[1] 3.2 kilometers
[2] 4 kilometers

2. VOCABULARY

Complete the sentences with the words below.

curious	famous	shivering	missing	amazed

1. Shiro disappeared. The Nakamuras looked everywhere for him, but they couldn't find him. Their dog was ___missing___.
2. Shiro always came back at night. He was wet and cold, so he was __________.
3. "Where does Shiro go?" Mr. Nakamura wondered. He wanted to know. One day he followed his dog because he was __________.
4. Shiro's swimming surprised people. "Nobody can swim from Aka to Zamami!" they said. People were __________ when they heard about Shiro.
5. A lot of people in Japan knew about Shiro. He became __________.

3. COMPREHENSION

UNDERSTANDING THE MAIN IDEA

Circle the letter of the best answer.

1. "Puppy Love" is about
a. two islands in Japan.
b. a Japanese holiday.
c. a dog who visits his girlfriend.

2. People were amazed when they heard about Shiro because
a. dogs don't usually fall in love.
b. swimming from Aka to Zamami is very difficult.
c. "Shiro" is an unusual name for a dog.

UNDERSTANDING CAUSE AND EFFECT

Find the best way to complete each sentence. Write the letter of your answer on the line.

1. Mr. and Mrs. Nakamura were worried __*c*__
2. Shiro was always wet when he came back ______
3. Mr. Nakamura followed Shiro ______
4. Shiro swam to Zamami ______
5. Three thousand people went to Zamami ______

a. because his girlfriend lived there.
b. because he was curious.
c. because their dog was missing.
d. because he swam in the ocean.
e. because they wanted to see Shiro.

REVIEWING THE STORY

Complete each sentence. Then read the story again and check your answers.

Mr. Nakamura was curious about his dog, Shiro. Shiro often ____*disappeared*____ (1) in the morning and ____________ (2) back late at night. He ____________ (3) always wet when he came back.

One morning Mr. Nakamura ____________ (4) Shiro. Shiro walked to the beach, ran into the water, and began to ____________ (5). He swam to Zamami, a Japanese island. Marilyn lived on Zamami. Marilyn was Shiro's

________________ (6).

People were amazed when they heard ________________ (7) Shiro. The

________________ (8) from Aka to Zamami is two and a half miles, and the

ocean between the islands is very ________________ (9).

Shiro became ________________ (10). Many people went to Zamami

because they wanted to see Shiro, the dog who was in ________________ (11).

4. DISCUSSION

Shiro is the Nakamuras' pet. Interview a classmate who has a pet. Ask your classmate the questions below. Listen carefully and write your classmate's answers. Then tell the class what you learned about your classmate's pet.

1. What kind of pet do you have? ________________

2. What is your pet's name? ________________

3. How old is your pet? ________________

4. Is your pet smart like Shiro? ________________

5. Does your pet do anything unusual? ________________

____

6. What do you like to do with your pet? ________________

7. Do you want more pets? ________________

5. WRITING

You can write a paragraph from your classmate's answers to the questions above. Here is what one student wrote.

Irma has a pet goldfish. His name is Tiger, and he is about one year old. Irma named her fish Tiger because he has stripes like a tiger. Tiger is not smart like Shiro. Tiger doesn't do anything unusual. He just swims around in his goldfish bowl. Maybe Irma will buy another goldfish. Then Tiger will have a friend.

Now write your paragraph on your own paper.

UNIT 2

1. PRE-READING

Look at the picture.

- What is the woman holding? Why do you think she is holding them?
- What is the man doing?

Read the title of the story. Look at the picture again.

- What do you think this story is about?
- Can you guess what happens?

Surprise! It's Your Wedding!

"Goodnight, John."

"Goodnight, Lynn."

Lynn Millington kissed her boyfriend goodnight. He walked to his car and drove away. Lynn walked into her house. It was midnight. Her parents were sleeping, and the house was quiet. Lynn sat down on the sofa. She had a problem, and she needed some time to think. Lynn's boyfriend was John Biggin. John loved Lynn, and Lynn loved John. They were very happy together. What was the problem? Lynn wanted to get married. John wanted to get married, too, but he was afraid.

Sometimes Lynn and John talked about getting married. "Let's get married in June," Lynn said. "June is a beautiful month for a wedding."

"June?" John asked. "This June? Let's not get married in June. Let's wait a little longer."

Lynn waited . . . and waited. She was very patient. She was patient, but she wanted to get married. Lynn's parents wanted her to get married, too; they liked John. John's parents also wanted them to get married because they liked Lynn. Suddenly Lynn had an idea. "John's parents will help me!" she thought.

The next morning Lynn telephoned John's parents. "I need your help," Lynn told them. "John wants to get married, but he's afraid. Let's plan a wedding for John and me. It will be this Saturday. Invite your family. But don't tell John about the wedding."

Next, Lynn telephoned Bob Raper. Bob was John's best friend. "I need your help," Lynn told Bob. "Tell John that you're getting married this Saturday. Invite him to your wedding." Bob wasn't really getting married on Saturday. It was a trick. John and Lynn were getting married on Saturday, but John didn't know it.

On Saturday morning John put on his best suit. Then he drove to the courthouse in Bridlington, England. He walked into the courthouse and looked around. He saw his friend Bob. He saw his girlfriend Lynn. Then he saw his parents, relatives, and friends. He saw Lynn's family and friends. Suddenly John understood. This was not Bob's wedding! This was John's wedding! John began to shake, but he didn't run away. Twenty minutes later John and Lynn were husband and wife.

After the wedding a photographer took pictures of John and Lynn. In one picture John is pretending to punch Lynn. He is pretending that he is angry. John is not really angry; he is smiling. Lynn, of course, is smiling, too.

2. VOCABULARY

Complete the sentences with the words below.

courthouse	patient	trick	wedding	punch

1. Lynn waited and waited. She was very ___patient___.
2. John's best friend, Bob, told him, "I'm getting married on Saturday." That wasn't true; Bob wasn't really getting married. It was a ________________.
3. John and Lynn live in England. In England, people get married at a church or at a ________________.
4. Lynn and Bob got married. After the ________________ a photographer took pictures.
5. In the picture on page 6, Bob is pretending to ________________ Lynn.

3. COMPREHENSION

UNDERSTANDING THE MAIN IDEA

Circle the letter of the best answer.

1. What was Lynn's problem?
a. John's parents didn't like her.
b. Lynn loved John's best friend.
c. John was afraid to get married.

2. John and Lynn's wedding was unusual because
a. Lynn didn't wear a white dress.
b. John didn't know about the wedding.
c. the wedding was at a courthouse.

UNDERSTANDING CONNECTIONS

Find the best way to complete each sentence. Write the letter of your answer on the line.

1. John wanted to get married, but __b__
2. Lynn was patient, but ______
3. Lynn told John's parents, "Invite your family to the wedding, but ______
4. When John understood that it was his wedding, he began to shake, but ______

a. don't tell John."
b. he was afraid.
c. he didn't run away.
d. she wanted to get married.

REMEMBERING DETAILS

Read the sentences. One word in each sentence is not correct. Find the word and cross it out. Write the correct word.

1. John loved Lynn and wanted to get married, but he was ~~angry.~~ afraid
2. Lynn told John's brothers, "I need your help."
3. "Let's plan a party for John and me," Lynn told John's parents.
4. Next, Lynn telephoned Bob Raper, who was John's boss.
5. She told him, "Tell John that you're getting married this Monday and invite him to the wedding."
6. Bob wasn't really getting married; it was a problem.

7. On Saturday morning John put on his best suit and drove to the library in Bridlington, England.
8. At the courthouse he telephoned Lynn, his friends, and his relatives.
9. Suddenly he understood: This was Bob's wedding!
10. Twenty minutes later John and Lynn were boyfriend and wife.

4. DISCUSSION

Read the sentences and circle *YES* or *NO*. Then read the sentences and your answers to a partner. Explain your answers to your partner.

1. I think John is happy that he married Lynn. **YES NO**
2. Lynn tricked John. I think that was a good idea. **YES NO**
3. In the picture, John is wearing a suit. Lynn is wearing a dress and she has flowers in her hair. In my native country, people sometimes dress like this for their wedding. **YES NO**
4. John is 24 years old. That is a good age for a man to get married. **YES NO**
5. I am (I was) afraid to get married. **YES NO**

5. WRITING

Is it better to be married or single? Fill in the chart below. Then discuss your answers with your classmates.

It is better to be married. Why?	It is better to be single. Why?
1. ______________________	1. ______________________
2. ______________________	2. ______________________
3. ______________________	3. ______________________

UNIT 3

1. PRE-READING

Look at the picture.

- What are the woman and the girl doing?
- How do you think they feel?
- What do you see behind them in the picture?

Read the title of the story. Look at the picture again.

- What do you think this story is about?
- Can you guess what happens?

The Train

On a warm spring afternoon, Nicole and her brother went outside to play. Nicole was eight, and her brother, Robert, was ten.

"Let's go to the bridge," Nicole said. "If we stand on the bridge, we can see fish in the river."

"I don't know . . . ," Robert said. "Mom told us, 'Don't go on the bridge.' She said it's dangerous."

"Oh, come on," Nicole said. "I'm not afraid. Are you?"

Nicole and Robert walked onto the bridge and began looking for fish in the river. The bridge was a train bridge. Three times a day, trains went over the bridge. But Nicole and Robert weren't thinking about trains. They were thinking about fish.

The children were standing in the middle of the bridge when they heard a loud noise. "A train's coming!" Robert yelled. "Run!" Robert ran to the end of the bridge. He was safe.

Nicole ran, too, but she fell. She got up and continued running. "Hurry! Hurry!" Robert yelled from the end of the bridge. "The train's coming!" Nicole looked behind her and saw the train. It was coming fast! Nicole ran toward her brother. Then she fell a second time. She fell right on the train track. She looked back again at the train. The train was very close now! There was no time to get up and run, so Nicole didn't move. She stayed where she was—lying between the rails of the train track. She put her head down and waited for the train to go over her. Robert stood at the end of the bridge and screamed.

A few seconds later, all twelve cars of the train went over Nicole. Sometimes the bottom of the train touched Nicole's back, but she was not hurt.

After the train went over her, Nicole stood up and yelled to Robert, "Don't tell Mom! Don't tell Mom!"

Of course, Nicole's mother found out about Nicole and the train. Nicole's mother was angry and happy at the same time. She was angry that Nicole went on the bridge, but she was happy that Nicole was alive.

And Nicole? How is she? Nicole's mother says, "Nicole is fine, but sometimes she goes to sleep and then wakes up crying. And she doesn't like the sound of trains."

2. VOCABULARY

Which sentence or picture has the same meaning as the sentence in the story? Circle the letter of your answer.

1. The children walked onto the *bridge* and began looking for fish in the river.

b.

2. "Run!" Robert *yelled*.

a. "Run!" Robert said quietly.
b. "Run!" Robert said loudly.

3. Nicole was lying *between the rails of the train track*.

a.

b.

4. Nicole doesn't like the *sound* of trains.

a. Nicole doesn't like to see trains.
b. Nicole doesn't like to hear trains.

3. COMPREHENSION

REMEMBERING DETAILS

One word in each sentence is not correct. Find the word and cross it out. Write the correct word.

1. On a warm winter afternoon, Nicole and her brother went outside to play.
2. Nicole was four years old, and her brother, Robert, was ten.
3. Nicole and Robert walked onto the bridge and began looking for rocks in the river.
4. Suddenly the children heard a quiet noise.
5. A truck was coming!
6. Robert walked to the end of the bridge; he was safe.
7. When Nicole fell the second time, there was no time to run, so she stayed where she was—sitting on the train track.
8. A few hours later, all twelve cars of the train went over Nicole.
9. Sometimes the top of the train touched Nicole's back, but she was not hurt.
10. After the train went over her, Nicole stood up and yelled to Robert, "Don't tell Dad!"

UNDERSTANDING CAUSE AND EFFECT

Find the best way to complete each sentence. Write the letter of your answer on the line.

1. Nicole and Robert went to the train bridge ______
2. The bridge was dangerous ______
3. When she fell the second time, Nicole didn't get up and run ______
4. Nicole told Robert, "Don't tell Mom" ______

a. because trains went over it three times a day.

b. because she thought, "Mom will be angry."

c. because they wanted to look for fish in the river.

d. because there was no time.

UNDERSTANDING A SUMMARY

Imagine this: You want to tell the story "The Train" to a friend. You want to tell the story quickly, in only five sentences. Which five sentences tell the story best? Check (✔) your answer.

1. ____ A girl and her brother were standing on a train bridge. They were looking for fish in the river. A train came. The boy ran to the end of the bridge and was safe, but the girl fell on the train track. The train went over her, but the girl was not hurt.

2. ____ A girl and her brother went outside to play. They walked onto a train bridge to look for fish in the river. Their mother had told them, "Don't go on the train bridge; it's dangerous." Three times a day, trains went over the bridge. But the children weren't thinking about trains; they were thinking about fish.

4. WRITING

The train bridge was dangerous, so Nicole's mother made a rule: "Don't go on the train bridge."

Parents everywhere have rules for their children. For example, they say, "Don't play with matches." "Be home before dark." "Wash your hands before you eat."

What rules did your parents have? Write your list below.

My parents told me:

____

____

____

____

____

____

5. DISCUSSION

Read the sentences you wrote above to a partner. Are your lists the same?

UNIT 4

1. PRE-READING

Look at the pictures.

- How old do you think the boy is?
- How old do you think the girl is?
- What is the girl holding?
- Can you read the words on the girl's T-shirt?

Read the title of the story. Look at the pictures again.

- What do you think this story is about?
- Can you guess what happens?

The Gift

Donna Ashlock, a 14-year-old girl from California, was very sick. She had a bad heart. "Donna needs a new heart," her doctors said. "She must have a new heart, or she will die soon."

Felipe Garza, 15, was worried about Donna. Felipe was Donna's friend. He liked Donna very much. He liked her freckles, and he liked her smile. Felipe didn't want Donna to die.

Felipe talked to his mother about Donna. "I'm going to die," Felipe told his mother, "and I'm going to give my heart to Donna."

Felipe's mother didn't pay much attention to Felipe. "Felipe is just kidding," she thought. "Felipe is not going to die. He's strong and healthy."

But Felipe was not healthy. He had terrible headaches sometimes. "My head really hurts," he often told his friends. Felipe never told his parents about his headaches.

One morning Felipe woke up with a sharp pain in his head. He was dizzy, and he couldn't breathe. The Garzas rushed Felipe to the hospital. Doctors at the hospital had terrible news for the Garzas. "Felipe's brain is dead," the doctors said. "We can't save him."

The Garzas were very sad. But they remembered Felipe's words. "Felipe wanted to give his heart to Donna," they told the doctors.

The doctors did several tests. Then they told the Garzas, "We can give Felipe's heart to Donna."

The doctors took out Felipe's heart and rushed the heart to Donna. Other doctors took out Donna's heart and put Felipe's heart in her chest. In a short time the heart began to beat.

The operation was a success. Felipe's heart was beating in Donna's chest, but Donna didn't know it. Her parents and doctors didn't tell her. They waited until she was stronger; then they told her about Felipe. "I feel very sad," Donna said, "but I'm thankful to Felipe."

Three months after the operation Donna Ashlock went back to school. She has to have regular checkups, and she has to take medicine every day. But she is living a normal life.

Felipe's brother John says, "Every time we see Donna, we think of Felipe. She has Felipe's heart in her. That gives us great peace."

2. VOCABULARY

Complete the sentences with the words below.

checkup	sharp	rushed	kidding	dizzy

1. When Felipe told his mother, "I'm going to die," she thought, "Felipe is not serious. He's only joking." She thought Felipe was just ___kidding___.
2. Felipe had a sudden, terrible pain in his head. It was a ______________ pain.
3. Felipe thought, "The room is going around and around." He felt ______________.
4. When Felipe's parents took him to the hospital, they drove fast. They ______________ him to the hospital.
5. Donna goes to the doctor sometimes. The doctor listens to her heart and makes sure it is working well. Donna goes to the doctor for a ______________.

3. COMPREHENSION

UNDERSTANDING THE MAIN IDEA

Circle the letter of the best answer.

1. The title of the story is "The Gift." What was the gift?

- **a.** the toys and balloons in the picture
- **b.** Felipe's heart
- **c.** the operation

2. Why did Donna feel sad and thankful?

- **a.** She had an operation, but she went back to school three months later.
- **b.** She has to take medicine every day, but she is living a normal life.
- **c.** Her friend Felipe died, but he gave Donna his heart.

UNDERSTANDING PRONOUNS

Look at the pronouns. What do they mean? Write the letter of your answer on the line.

1. __e__ *They* said Donna needed a new heart.

2. ______ *He* was Donna's friend.

3. ______ Felipe told *them* his head hurt.

4. ______ *They* told the doctors, "Felipe wanted to give his heart to Donna."

5. ______ *It* was a success.

6. ______ Donna has to take *it* every day.

- **a.** Felipe Garza
- **b.** Felipe's friends
- **c.** medicine
- **d.** the Garzas
- **e.** doctors
- **f.** Donna's operation

FINDING MORE INFORMATION

Read each sentence on the left. Which sentence on the right gives you more information? Match the sentences. Write the letter of your answer on the line.

1. __d__ Donna Ashlock was *very sick.*

2. ______ Felipe was *not healthy.*

3. ______ Doctors at the hospital had *terrible news* for the Garzas.

4. ______ The Garzas remembered *Felipe's words.*

- **a.** He had terrible headaches sometimes.
- **b.** "I'm going to give my heart to Donna."
- **c.** "We can't save Felipe," they said.
- **d.** She had a bad heart.

4. DISCUSSION

Many people carry donor cards in their wallets. A donor card says, "If I die in an accident, take my heart and other important organs. Give them to sick people."

Do you want a donor card? Check (✔) your answer.

____ Yes

____ No

____ I'm not sure.

In a small group, explain your answer.

5. WRITING

The title of the story is "The Gift." Would you like a gift? Imagine this: One day you come home from English class and walk into the kitchen. A big box is on the kitchen table. The box has your name on it. It's a gift for you! You open the box and look at your gift. It is something you have wanted for a long, long time.

What is your gift? Write about it. Here is an example.

When I walked into the kitchen, I smelled something delicious. It smelled like food from my country. "That's impossible!" I thought. Then I saw the box and opened it. Inside the box was a dinner with my favorite foods. My mother sent the dinner from Panama! The dinner was rice, beans, and ceviche. (Ceviche is seafood with lemon, garlic, and onions; it is very spicy.) I ate the dinner. It was delicious. Thank you, Mom!

UNIT 5

1. PRE-READING

Look at the picture.

- How old do you think the boy is?
- What is he doing?

Read the title of the story. Look at the picture again.

- What do you think the boy did?
- Can you guess what happens?

Oh Boy, What a Ride!

Robert Vogel is a police officer in Rye, New York. One morning Officer Vogel was drinking coffee in a restaurant. He was on his coffee break. Suddenly the doors of the restaurant opened, and a man ran in. "Officer!" the man yelled. "A car is going down the street—and a little kid is driving it!"

Officer Vogel ran out of the restaurant. He saw a station wagon. It was going slowly—about 25 miles[1] an hour—but it wasn't going very straight. He jumped into his police car and followed the station wagon. When he was behind it, he turned on his red light and siren. The station wagon moved to the side of the road and stopped.

Officer Vogel got out of his police car, hurried to the station wagon, and looked inside. The driver was a little boy. His name was Rocco Morabito, and he was five years old. In the back seat was Rocco's little sister. She was only two years old. Both children were crying.

"I want my Mommy!" Rocco cried. "But she can't get here. I have the car." Then Rocco had an idea. "Just a minute," he told Officer Vogel. "I can drive. I'll go get her."

"No!" Officer Vogel said. "You stay with me!"

Officer Vogel drove Rocco and his sister to the police station. Then he called their mother. Officer Vogel and Rocco's mother had a lot of questions for Rocco. Their first question was: "Where did you get the car keys?"

Rocco said, "From the top of the refrigerator." At seven o'clock that morning Rocco's father was at work and his mother was sleeping. Rocco saw the car keys on top of the refrigerator. He pulled a chair over to the refrigerator, climbed up on the chair, and took the keys.

Rocco went to the garage and got into the car. Then he started the engine. When Rocco's sister heard the engine, she ran to the car and began to cry. She wanted to go with him, so Rocco opened the back door and let her in the car.

Rocco backed the car out of the garage and drove away. It was 7 A.M.—rush hour—so there was a lot of traffic. Rocco drove one mile[2] in heavy traffic. Then Officer Vogel stopped him.

Newspapers and TV stations heard about Rocco, and a lot of reporters went to his house. One reporter asked Rocco, "What do you want to be when you grow up?"

Rocco smiled. "I want to be a truck driver," he said.

[1] 40 kilometers
[2] 1.6 kilometers

2. VOCABULARY

Complete the sentences with the words below.

heavy	coffee break	siren	rush hour	station wagon

1. Officer Vogel stopped working for 15 minutes. He went to a restaurant to drink a cup of coffee. He was on his ___*coffee break*___.
2. Rocco drove a big car with seats for nine people. It was a ______________.
3. Rocco drove the car at 7 A.M. Many people were driving to work. It was ______________.
4. There were a lot of cars on the road. Traffic was ______________.
5. Rocco stopped the car because he heard the ______________ on the police car.

3. COMPREHENSION

UNDERSTANDING THE MAIN IDEA

Circle the letter of the best answer.

1. This story is about
- **a.** a police officer.
- **b.** a little boy who drove a car.
- **c.** safe driving in New York.

2. The story has a happy ending because
- **a.** Rocco was a very good driver.
- **b.** Rocco didn't have an accident.
- **c.** Rocco wants to be a truck driver.

UNDERSTANDING REASONS

Find the best way to complete each sentence. Write the letter of your answer on the line.

1. Officer Vogel went to a restaurant ______

2. Rocco climbed up on a chair ______

3. Rocco opened the back door ______

4. Officer Vogel called Rocco's mother ______

5. Reporters went to Rocco's house ______

a. to get the car keys.

b. to ask him questions.

c. to let his sister in the car.

d. to drink a cup of coffee.

e. to tell her, "Your son is at the police station."

REMEMBERING DETAILS

Read the sentences. One word in each sentence is not correct. Find the word and cross it out. Write the correct word.

police officer

1. Robert Vogel is a ~~salesman~~ in Rye, New York.

2. One evening he was drinking coffee in a restaurant.

3. Suddenly the doors of the restaurant opened, and a woman ran in.

4. The man yelled, "A car is going down the street—and a little kid is fixing it!"

5. Officer Vogel jumped into his police car and hit the station wagon.

6. The driver's name was Rocco Morabito, and he was 50 years old.

7. Rocco took the car keys from the top of the television.
8. Rocco opened the back seat and let his sister in the car.
9. Rocco drove one mile in light traffic.
10. A lot of mechanics went to Rocco's house.

4. DISCUSSION

The reporters asked Rocco, "What do you want to be when you grow up?" He answered, "I want to be a truck driver."

When you were a child, what did you want to be when you grew up? (For example: a doctor, a soccer player, a homemaker) What do you want to be now? (or What are you now?)

First, answer the questions yourself. Then ask three classmates the questions. Write their answers in the chart.

	When you were a child, what did you want to be?	**What do you want to be now? or What are you now?**
Your name		
Classmate's name		
Classmate's name		
Classmate's name		

What did you learn about your classmates? Tell the class.

5. WRITING

When Officer Vogel went back to the police station, he had to write a report. This is how he began his report:

At 7 A.M. I was drinking coffee at the Coffee Cup restaurant . . .

Finish Officer Vogel's report on your own paper.

UNIT 6

1. PRE-READING

Look at the picture.

- Where do you think these people are from?
- How old do you think this photo is?
- What is unusual about the two men in the center of the photo?

Read the title of the story. Look at the picture again.

- What do you think this story is about?
- Can you guess what happens?

The Twins of Siam

A young mother was lying on a bed. She had just given birth to twin boys. She was tired but happy. A woman was helping her. Suddenly the woman screamed. "What's the matter?" the mother cried. She lifted her head and looked at her babies. The babies were joined at their chests. She could not separate them.

That happened in Siam—now called Thailand—in 1811. The mother named her babies Chang and Eng. Chang and Eng grew up and became the famous Siamese twins.

People came from all over Siam to stare at the twins. One day, when the twins were 18, an American saw them. He thought, "I can make money with the twins." He asked Chang and Eng, "Will you come with me to the United States?" Chang and Eng wanted to go to the United States, so they went with the man. They never saw Siam or their family again.

Chang and Eng traveled with the American for ten years. Later they traveled alone. People paid to see them and ask them questions about their lives. Finally, the twins got tired of traveling. They got tired of answering questions. They decided to live quietly in North Carolina.

Soon after they moved to North Carolina, the twins met two sisters. The sisters' names were Adelaide and Sarah. The twins fell in love with the sisters. Chang married Adelaide, and Eng married Sarah. The marriages were very unusual. Adelaide and Sarah lived in separate houses. The twins lived in one house for four days. Then they went to the other house for four days. The marriages were unusual, but they were long and happy. Chang and Adelaide had ten children, and Eng and Sarah had eleven children.

The twins were happy with Adelaide and Sarah, but they were not always happy with each other. Sometimes they argued, and they didn't talk to each other. They asked doctor after doctor, "Please separate us." Every doctor said, "I can't separate you. The operation is too dangerous." So, the twins stayed joined together.

One night, when the twins were 63, Eng suddenly woke up. He looked at Chang, who was lying beside him. Chang was not breathing. Eng screamed for help, and one of his sons came.

"Uncle Chang is dead," the young man said.

"Then I am going to die, too," Eng said, and he began to cry. Two hours later Eng was dead.

For 63 years the twins of Siam lived together as one. In the end, they also died as one.

2. VOCABULARY

Read the sentences. Guess the meaning of the words. Circle the letter of your answer.

1. A woman was helping the young mother. Suddenly the woman *screamed.* "What's the matter?" the mother cried.

a. yelled in a loud voice
b. smiled happily

2. The babies were joined at their chests. She could not *separate* them.

a. take them apart
b. wake them up

3. People came from all over Siam to *stare at* the twins.

a. take pictures of
b. look at

4. The twins were not always happy with each other. Sometimes they *argued.*

a. spoke quietly
b. spoke in angry voices

3. COMPREHENSION

UNDERSTANDING THE MAIN IDEA

Circle the letter of the best answer.

1. This story is about
- **a.** dangerous operations.
- **b.** unusual marriages.
- **c.** Siamese twin brothers.

2. The twins talked to many doctors because
- **a.** the twins were often sick.
- **b.** they wanted the doctors to separate them.
- **c.** the doctors wanted to study the twins.

REMEMBERING DETAILS

Read the sentences. One word in each sentence is not correct. Find the word and cross it out. Write the correct word.

Thailand

1. The story happened in Siam—now called ~~China~~ —in 1811.

2. Chang and Eng grew up and became the famous Siamese doctors.

3. People came from all over Siam to laugh at the twins.

4. An Australian asked Chang and Eng to come with him to the United States.

5. Chang and Eng traveled with the American for ten days.

6. After they moved to North Carolina, the twins met two cousins.

7. The marriages were unusual, but they were long and unhappy.

8. Every doctor said, "I can separate you because the operation is too dangerous."

UNDERSTANDING REASONS

Find the best way to complete each sentence. Write the letter of your answer on the line.

1. The young mother lifted her head ______

2. Chang and Eng went to the United States ______

3. People paid ______

4. The twins went to doctor after doctor ______

a. to ask the twins questions.

b. to ask about an operation.

c. to travel with the American.

d. to look at her babies.

4. DISCUSSION

The twins of Siam were famous. People paid to see them and ask them questions about their lives.

Play the game "Twenty Questions" with your classmates.

Think of a famous person, living or dead. Tell your teacher who you are thinking of, but don't tell your classmates. Then sit in front of the class. Your classmates will ask you questions, and you will answer only "yes" or "no." Can your classmates guess who you are in fewer than 20 questions? Here are some sample questions:

- Are you a woman?
- Are you alive?
- Are you an actor?
- Are you rich?
- Did you live a long time ago?
- Are you a political leader?
- Are you French?
- Are you an athlete?
- Are you a singer?
- Are you handsome?

5. WRITING

The twins married two sisters. Their marriages were happy. Not all marriages are happy every day.

Look at the picture of a husband and wife. Why is the husband angry? What is he saying? Write it.

Look at the next picture. Why is the wife angry? What is she saying? Write it.

What did you write? Tell your classmates.

UNIT 7

1. PRE-READING

Look at the picture.

- Why do you think the women are smiling?
- How old do you think the babies are?

Read the title of the story. Look at the picture again.

- What do you think this story is about?
- Can you guess what happens?

The Baby Exchange

Selma Scarausi looked at her baby daughter and smiled. The baby smiled back. Selma began to cry. "I love my baby very much," Selma thought. "But is she really my baby?"

Selma's baby was born at a hospital in Sao Paulo, Brazil. A few days later Selma and the baby came home from the hospital. Friends and relatives were surprised when they saw the baby. The baby didn't look like her parents. The baby had dark skin and curly hair, but Selma and her husband had light skin and straight hair. "Babies change," everyone thought. "She will look like her parents when she is older."

But the baby didn't change. When she was nine months old, she still looked very different from her parents. Selma and her husband, Paulo, took the baby back to the hospital. "Are you sure this is our baby?" they asked the hospital director.

"Of course she is your baby," the director said. "Immediately after the babies are born, we give them bracelets with numbers. Your baby was number 51. You left the hospital with baby 51. A mistake is impossible."

"A mistake *is* possible," Selma and Paulo thought. "We have another family's baby. And somewhere another family has our baby. But Sao Paulo is a city of seven million people. How can we find our baby?"

Selma and Paulo went to the hospital again. A nurse at the hospital told Paulo, "I remember another couple. Their baby didn't look like them. The parents had dark skin, but the baby had light skin. The father had very curly hair, but the baby had straight hair." The nurse gave Paulo the couple's address.

The next day Selma took her baby to the couple's house. She knocked, and a woman opened the door. The woman took one look at Selma's baby and fainted. Selma helped her into the house. There, in the living room, was a nine-month-old baby. Selma knew that the baby was hers.

Selma and Paulo's baby was living with Maria and Luiz Souza. The Souzas also had wondered about their baby because she looked so different from them. When Maria Souza saw the baby in Selma's arms, she, too, knew the baby was hers.

The hospital made a mistake. Both babies were born at the hospital on the same day. The hospital gave both babies the number 51.

During the next weeks the two families prepared to exchange babies. First they exchanged information about the babies' habits. Then they exchanged toys and clothes. Finally, with smiles and tears, they exchanged babies.

2. VOCABULARY

Which picture or words have the same meaning as the sentences in the story? Circle the letter of your answer.

1. Immediately after the babies are born, we give them *bracelets* with numbers.

a. 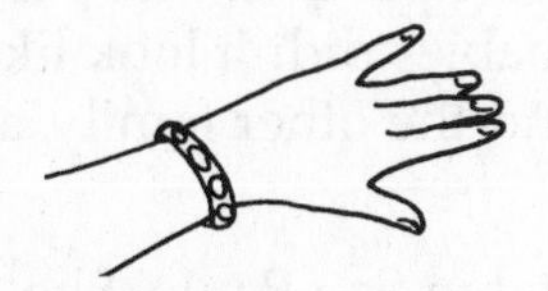

b. 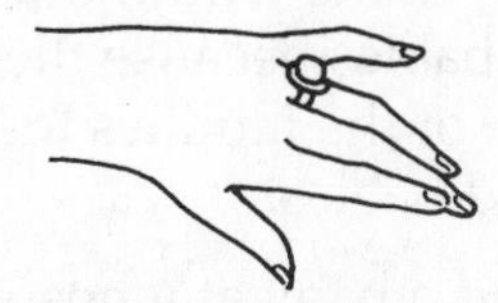

2. Maria Souza took one look at Selma's baby and *fainted.*

a. left the house with the baby
b. fell to the floor and didn't move

3. The two families exchanged information about the babies' *habits.*

a. things people do every day
b. places people like to go

4. Finally, with smiles and *tears,* they exchanged babies.

a. water that comes from people's eyes when they cry
b. gifts that people give to babies

3. COMPREHENSION

UNDERSTANDING THE MAIN IDEA

Circle the letter of the best answer.

1. The story is about
   a. the city of Sao Paulo, Brazil.
   b. two couples who got the wrong babies.
   c. babies' habits, toys, and clothes.

2. Selma and Paulo thought, "We have the wrong baby" because
   a. hospitals sometimes make mistakes.
   b. they wanted a son, not a daughter.
   c. their baby didn't look like them.

UNDERSTANDING CAUSE AND EFFECT

Find the best way to complete each sentence. Write the letter of your answer on the line.

1. Friends and relatives were surprised _____
2. Selma and Paulo went back to the hospital _____
3. The hospital director said that a mistake was impossible _____
4. It was difficult for Selma and Paulo to find their baby _____
5. Maria Souza fainted _____

a. because Sao Paulo is a big city.
b. because she knew that the baby in Selma's arms was her baby.
c. because they thought they had the wrong baby.
d. because the hospital gave each baby a number.
e. because the baby didn't look like her parents.

UNDERSTANDING A SUMMARY

Imagine this: You want to tell the story "The Baby Exchange" to a friend. You want to tell the story quickly, in only four sentences. Which four sentences tell the story best? Check (✔) your answer.

1. _____ There was a mistake at a hospital in Brazil. Two babies were born on the same day and went home with the wrong parents. The parents wondered about their babies because the babies didn't look like them. Nine months later, one of the families found the other family, and the two families exchanged babies.

2. _____ A Brazilian woman had a baby at a hospital in Sao Paulo. She wondered about her baby because the baby didn't look like her or her husband. When the baby was nine months old, the woman and her husband took their baby to the hospital. They asked the hospital director, "Are you sure this is our baby?"

4. DISCUSSION

Before the families exchanged babies, they exchanged information about the babies' habits. What habits do the people in your class have? Find out.

First, count off (1, 2, 3, 4 . . .) until everyone in the class has a number. Write your number on a piece of paper and tape it to your shirt. Now look for your number in the list below. Look at the question next to your number. That is *your* question.

1. Do you sleep in the afternoon?
2. Do you sing in the shower?
3. Do you exercise?
4. Do you wear a ring?
5. Do you bite your nails?
6. Do you come to class late?
7. Do you walk fast?
8. Do you wear a watch?
9. Do you sleep with two pillows?
10. Do you go to bed after midnight?
11. Do you have a comb in your pocket or purse?
12. Do you fall asleep when you watch TV?
13. Do you read before you go to sleep?
14. Do you drink coffee in the morning?
15. Do you spend a lot of money on phone calls?
16. Do you make your bed every day?
17. Do you bring a notebook to English class?
18. Do you sing when you drive a car?
19. Do you pick up coins you find on the street?

Write your question at the top of a piece of paper. Write numbers under the question, as many numbers as there are people in your class. Then walk around the room. Ask people your question. Write each person's answer next to his or her number. For example:

Do you sleep in the afternoon?
1. Yes
2. No, never
3. Sometimes, if I am really tired

After you ask everyone your question and write their answers, report back to the class. Tell the class what you learned. For example:

"Only four people always sleep in the afternoon. Two people sometimes sleep in the afternoon. The rest of the class never sleeps in the afternoon."

5. WRITING

Think about your family and friends. Do they have any habits that you don't like—habits that make you a little angry? Write about them. For example:

- *When we go somewhere, my mother always loses something.*
- *My friend eats a banana like a monkey.*

Now write your sentences on your own paper.

UNIT 8

1. PRE-READING

Look at the picture.

- What is the man doing?

Read the title of the story. Look at the picture again.

- What do you think this story is about?
- What do you think the man wants to do?

Why Can't They Quit?

The man in the picture is Ali. Ali is from Saudi Arabia, but he is living in the United States. Ali will stay in the United States for one year. During the year, Ali wants to do two things. First, he wants to learn English. Second, he wants to quit smoking.

Ali has smoked for nine years. He smokes a pack of cigarettes every day. Ali says, "I tried to quit smoking in Saudi Arabia, but it was impossible. My brothers smoke. All my friends smoke. At parties and at meetings, almost all the men smoke. Here in the United States, not as many people smoke. It will be easier to quit here."

Many smokers are like Ali: they want to quit smoking. They know that smoking is bad for their health. They know it can cause cancer and heart disease. But it is difficult for them to stop smoking because cigarettes have a drug in them. The drug is nicotine. People who smoke a lot need nicotine.

The first few times a person smokes, the smoker usually feels terrible. The nicotine makes the person sick. In a few days, the smoker's body gets used to the nicotine, and the smoker feels fine. Later, the smoker needs nicotine to feel fine. Without it, the smoker feels terrible. The smoker is addicted to nicotine.

What happens when people quit smoking? What happens when smokers don't have nicotine? People who quit smoking are often depressed and nervous for weeks. Some people eat instead of smoking, so they gain weight.

Doctors sometimes give special chewing gum to people who want to quit smoking. The chewing gum has a little nicotine in it. When smokers need nicotine, they don't smoke cigarettes. They chew the gum instead. Each day the smokers try to chew the gum less often. With the gum, people can quit smoking and then gradually give up nicotine.

It is very difficult to quit smoking, and many people who quit will smoke again. At a party or maybe at work they will decide to smoke "just one" cigarette. Then they will smoke another cigarette, and another. Soon they are smokers again. Maybe there is only one easy way to quit smoking: never start.

2. VOCABULARY

Complete the sentences with the words below.

get used to	pack	quit	causes

1. Ali tried to stop smoking in Saudi Arabia, but it was impossible. He hopes it will be easier to ____quit____ smoking in the United States.

2. There are 20 cigarettes in a ____________________.

3. Sometimes people who smoke have cancer or bad hearts because smoking ____________________ these diseases.

4. When people smoke for the first time, the nicotine makes them sick. In a few days they feel fine because their bodies ____________________ the nicotine.

3. COMPREHENSION

UNDERSTANDING THE MAIN IDEA

Circle the letter of the best answer.

1. It is difficult to quit smoking because

a. a lot of people smoke at parties and meetings.
b. many people who quit will smoke again.
c. smokers are addicted to nicotine.

2. Nicotine is

a. a kind of chewing gum.
b. a drug in cigarettes.
c. a popular food in Saudi Arabia.

FINDING MORE INFORMATION

Read each sentence on the left. Which sentences on the right give you more information? Write the letter of your answer on the line.

1. ______ Ali wants to do *two things.*

2. ______ Ali *smokes.*

3. ______ Smoking is *bad* for the smoker's health.

4. ______ There is a *special chewing gum* for people who want to quit smoking.

a. It can cause cancer and heart disease.

b. It has a little nicotine in it. People chew the gum instead of smoking.

c. First, he wants to learn English. Second, he wants to quit smoking.

d. He smokes a pack of cigarettes every day.

REVIEWING THE STORY

Complete each sentence. Then read the story again and check your answers.

It is difficult to quit smoking because smokers are ____addicted____ (1) to nicotine. Nicotine is a ______________ (2) that is in cigarettes.

People who quit ______________ (3) are often depressed and nervous. Some people gain ______________ (4) because they eat instead of smoking.

People who want to quit smoking sometimes chew a special ______________ (5). The gum has a ______________ (6) nicotine in it. When smokers need nicotine, they ______________ (7) the gum.

It is very difficult to ______(8)______ smoking, and many people who quit will ______(9)______ again. Maybe there is only one easy ______(10)______ to quit smoking: never start.

4. DISCUSSION

Read the sentences and circle *YES* or *NO*. Then take turns reading the sentences and your answers to a partner. Explain your answers to your partner.

1.	A lot of men in my native country smoke.	**YES**	**NO**
2.	A lot of women in my native country smoke.	**YES**	**NO**
3.	A lot of children in my native country smoke.	**YES**	**NO**
4.	In my native country, smoking is not allowed in some places.	**YES**	**NO**
5.	I smoke a little.	**YES**	**NO**
6.	I smoke a lot.	**YES**	**NO**
7.	I began smoking when I was young.	**YES**	**NO**
8.	I used to smoke, but I quit.	**YES**	**NO**
9.	I have never smoked a cigarette.	**YES**	**NO**
10.	I think cigarette smoke smells good.	**YES**	**NO**

5. WRITING

Many people think smoking is a bad habit. There are other bad habits. Some people, for example, drink too much coffee. Some people watch too much TV.

What are your bad habits—habits you want to stop? What are your good habits—habits you want to keep? Make two lists.

MY BAD HABITS

1. ______________________________
2. ______________________________

MY GOOD HABITS

1. ______________________________
2. ______________________________

UNIT 9

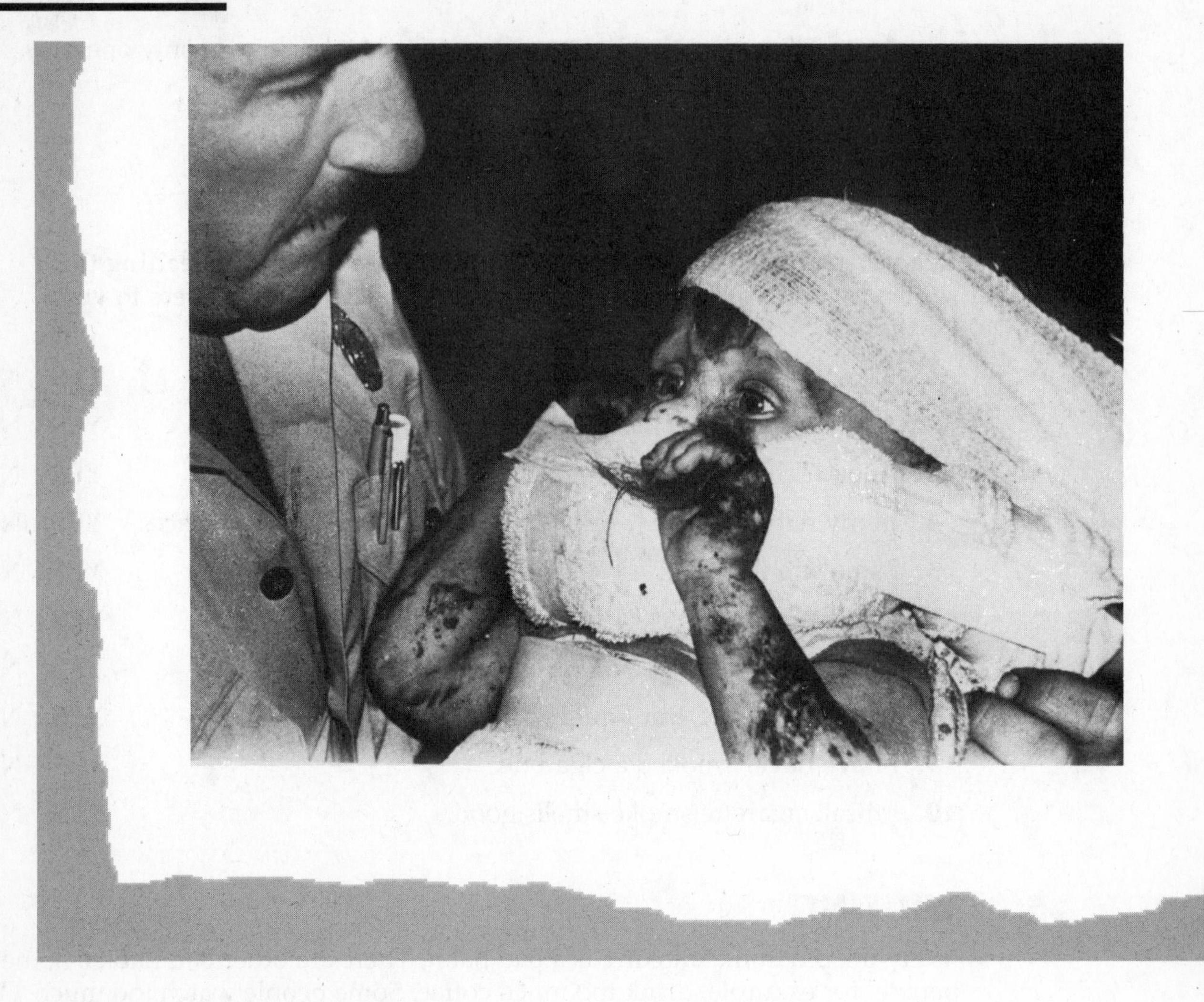

1. PRE-READING

Look at the picture.

- How old is the little girl?
- How do you think she feels?
- What does she have around her head?
- Who is holding the little girl?

Read the title of the story. Look at the picture again.

- What do you think this story is about?
- Can you guess what happened?

Everybody's Baby

At a day care center in Texas, children were playing outside. One of the children was Jessica McClure. She was 18 months old. Jessica's mother, who worked at the day care center, was watching the children. Suddenly Jessica fell and disappeared. Jessica's mother screamed and ran to her.

A well was in the yard of the day care center. The well was only eight inches across, and a rock always covered it. But children had moved the rock. When Jessica fell, she fell right into the well.

Jessica's mother reached inside the well, but she couldn't feel Jessica. She ran to a phone and dialed 911 for help.

Men from the fire department arrived. They discovered that Jessica was about 20 feet[1] down in the well. For the next hour the men talked and planned Jessica's rescue. Then they told Jessica's parents their plan.

"We can't go down into the well," they said. "It's too narrow. So, we're going to drill a hole next to the well. We'll drill down about 20 feet. Then we'll drill a tunnel across to Jessica. When we reach her, we'll bring her through the tunnel. Then we'll bring her up through our hole."

The men began to drill the hole on a Wednesday morning. "We'll reach Jessica in a few hours," they thought. The men were wrong. They had to drill through solid rock. Two days later, on Friday morning, they were still drilling. And Jessica McClure was still in the well.

During her days in the well, Jessica sometimes called for her mother. Sometimes she slept, sometimes she cried, and sometimes she sang.

All over the world people waited for news of Jessica. They read about her in newspapers and watched her rescue on TV. Everyone worried about the little girl in the well.

At 8 P.M. on Friday, the men finally reached Jessica and brought her up from the well. Then paramedics rushed her to the hospital. Jessica was dirty, hungry, thirsty, and tired. Her foot and forehead were badly injured. But Jessica was alive. A doctor at the hospital said, "Jessica is lucky she's very young. She's not going to remember this very well."

Maybe Jessica will not remember her days in the well. But her parents, her rescuers, and many other people around the world will not forget them.

After Jessica's rescue, one of the rescuers made a metal cover for the well. On the cover he wrote, "To Jessica, with love from all of us."

[1] 6 meters

2. VOCABULARY

Complete the sentences with the words below.

drill	narrow	injured	day care center	dialed

1. Jessica's mother took care of small children. She worked at a *day care center*.
2. The well was only eight inches across. It was ____________________.
3. After Jessica fell into the well, her mother ran to the phone and ____________________ 911.
4. The men used machines to ____________________ a hole next to the well.
5. Paramedics rushed Jessica to the hospital. Her foot and forehead were badly ____________________.

3. COMPREHENSION

UNDERSTANDING THE MAIN IDEA

Circle the letter of the best answer.

1. This story is about
 a. day care centers in Texas.
 b. the rescue of a little girl.
 c. drilling wells.

2. The story has a happy ending because
 a. Jessica was very young.
 b. Jessica was in the well only two days.
 c. the men rescued Jessica.

UNDERSTANDING TIME RELATIONSHIPS

Find the best way to complete each sentence. Write the letter of your answer on the line.

1. When Jessica fell, ______

2. When Jessica's mother reached inside the well, ______

3. When the men from the fire department arrived, ______

4. When Jessica was in the well, ______

5. When the rescuers reached Jessica, ______

a. she slept, cried, and sang.

b. they brought her through the tunnel and then up through their hole.

c. she couldn't feel Jessica.

d. she fell right into the well.

e. they discovered that Jessica was about 20 feet down in the well.

REMEMBERING DETAILS

Read the sentences. One word in each sentence is not correct. Find the word and cross it out. Write the correct word.

months

1. Jessica McClure was 18 ~~years~~ old.

2. A well was in the kitchen of the day care center.

3. When Jessica fell, she fell right into the water.

4. Jessica's mother ran to a phone and wrote 911.

5. The men said, "We're going to drill a cover next to the well."

6. The men had to drill through soft rock.

7. At 8 P.M. on Friday, men reached Jessica and brought her down from the well.
8. Then doctors rushed her to the hospital.
9. A doctor at the hospital said, "Jessica is lucky she's very old."
10. After Jessica's rescue a worker made a metal rock for the well.

4. DISCUSSION

The doctor said, "Jessica is lucky she's very young. She's not going to remember this very well."

Think back to the time when you were very young. Is there an experience you remember? Can you draw a picture of it?

Here is what one student drew. What do you think this student's experience was?

Now draw your picture on your own paper. Show your drawing to a small group of classmates. Tell the people in your group about your experience.

5. WRITING

Read this story. It is in the present. Write the story again in the past.

Jessica is playing at a day care center. Suddenly she falls into a well. She falls about 20 feet and can't get out of the well.

Men from the fire department come. They can't go down into the well because it is too narrow. The men decide to drill a hole next to the well.

For the next 58 hours the men drill the hole. Their job is very difficult because they are drilling through solid rock. Finally they reach Jessica and bring her up from the well. Jessica's foot and forehead are badly injured, but she is alive. Everyone is very happy.

Jessica was playing at a day care center. . . .

UNIT 10

1. PRE-READING

Look at the picture.

- Where are these people?
- What is on the shelves behind the man?
- What is the man doing?

Read the title of the story. Look at the picture again.

- What do you think this story is about?

Please Pass the Bird Brains

Do you have a headache? Eat some bird brains for dinner, and your headache will go away. Do you want beautiful skin? Put a spoonful of ground pearls into your soup. Your skin will be beautiful. Is your hair turning gray? Eat black rice every day, and you won't have gray hair.

"Eat bird brains, pearls, and black rice?" some people ask. "How strange!" But for many Chinese people, bird brains, pearls, and black rice are not strange things to eat; they are good things to eat. They are good medicines, too.

Many Chinese believe that food can be medicine. They believe that eating bird brains, for example, stops headaches, soup with ground pearls is good for the skin, and black rice stops hair from turning gray.

Food that is medicine is called medicinal food. The Chinese have eaten medicinal food and spices for centuries. Ginger, for example, is a common spice in Chinese cooking. Ginger gives food a nice flavor. The Chinese began to use ginger many years ago. They used ginger not because it tasted good. They used ginger because it was medicinal. Ginger, they thought, was good for the digestion. It also helped people who had colds. Pepper and garlic, too, were probably medicines a long time ago.

Some people don't believe that food and spices are good medicines. They want to buy their medicine in drug stores, not in supermarkets. Other people want to try medicinal food. They say, "Maybe medicinal food can't help me. But it can't hurt me, either."

People can try medicinal food at a Chinese restaurant in San Francisco, California. The restaurant serves only medicinal food. The menus at the restaurant have a list of dinners. Next to each dinner, there is information about the food . The information helps people order. "Queen's Secret," for example, is one dinner at the restaurant. Meat from a chicken with black skin is in the dinner. It is for women who want to look young. "Lover's Soup" is for people whose marriages are unhappy. The soup has dinosaur bones in it, and it helps people's love lives. Even the drinks at the restaurant are medicinal. One drink is deer tail wine. It gives people more energy.

Alan Lau is the owner of the restaurant. Mr. Lau says, "Some people try medicinal food one time and then say, 'It didn't work.' But think about this: When your doctor prescribes medicine, you take the medicine for five days, or for ten days, or maybe for weeks. It's the same with medicinal food. You have to eat the food many times before it begins to help." Mr. Lau believes that medicinal food works; he eats medicinally every day.

Mr. Lau also owns a store that sells medicinal food. The store is next to the restaurant. People who want to cook medicinal food at home can buy it at the store. In the picture, Mr. Lau is working at his store. He is weighing something for a customer. Is it a spice? Is it medicine? Or is it both?

2. VOCABULARY

Complete the sentences with the words below.

centuries	common	ground	digestion

1. For beautiful skin, some people eat very, very small pieces of pearls. They put *ground* pearls in their soup.
2. The Chinese have eaten medicinal food for hundreds of years. They have eaten medicinal food for ______________.
3. The Chinese use ginger often. It is a ______________ spice in Chinese cooking.
4. Ginger helps the stomach. It is good for the ______________.

3. COMPREHENSION

UNDERSTANDING THE MAIN IDEA

Circle the letter of the best answer.

1. "Please Pass the Bird Brains" is about

a. eating bird brains.
b. Chinese medicinal food.
c. delicious food and spices.

2. People who like medicinal food say,

a. "Food and spices can be good medicine."
b. "I buy medicine only in drug stores."
c. "Eating bird brains is strange."

REMEMBERING DETAILS

Read the sentences. One word in each sentence is not correct. Find the word and cross it out. Write the correct word.

1. Many Chinese people believe that ~~furniture~~ food can be medicine.
2. Eating bird brains stops backaches.
3. Soup with ground beef is good for the skin.
4. Black rice stops hair from turning red.
5. Food that is medicine is called delicious food.
6. The Chinese have eaten medicinal food for months.
7. Ginger, pepper, and garlic were medicines a short time ago.
8. People can try medicinal food at a bakery in San Francisco.

FINDING MORE INFORMATION

Read each sentence on the left. Which sentences on the right give you more information? Match the sentences. Write the letter of your answer on the line.

1. __d__ Many Chinese believe that *food can be medicine.*

2. ______ *Ginger* is a common spice in Chinese cooking.

3. ______ The menus at the restaurant give *information* about the food.

4. ______ Mr. Lau also owns a *store* that sells medicinal food.

a. It is next to the restaurant.

b. It gives food a nice flavor, and it is good for the digestion.

c. One dinner, "Queen's Secret," is for women who want to look young.

d. For example, soup with ground pearls is good for the skin.

4. DISCUSSION

Not only the Chinese use medicinal food. People all over the world use medicinal food and home remedies. For example, when someone has an earache, people in Italy put a little warm olive oil in the ear. Putting olive oil in the ear is a home remedy for an earache. Do your classmates use medicinal food and home remedies?

Ask a classmate: Do you know any home remedies for these problems?

- an earache
- a cold
- a sore throat
- a headache
- a stomachache
- a burn
- hiccups

Share information about medicinal food and home remedies with the class.

5. WRITING

Imagine this: There is a special medicinal food. It is not for headaches or stomachaches. This medicinal food is for problems. When you eat it, your problems go away. You go to the store, buy the medicinal food, and eat it.

Which problems go away? Write about them. Here is an example.

I had three problems. My English was not good. I didn't have enough money. I didn't have a boyfriend. Then I ate the medicinal food. Now my English is perfect. I got a new job, and I make $50,000 a year. I have plenty of money. I also have a boyfriend. He is very handsome. That medicinal food was great!

UNIT 11

I. PRE-READING

Look at the picture.

- What is unusual about the way the women are playing the piano?
- Why do you think they are playing the piano together?

Read the title of the story. Look at the picture again.

- Do you think the women are old friends or new friends?
- What do you think this story is about?
- Can you guess what happens?

Margaret Patrick . . . Meet Ruth Eisenberg

Ruth Eisenberg and Margaret Patrick play the piano. They give concerts in the United States and in Canada, and they are often on TV. They are famous.

Why are these women famous? They play the piano well, but they are not famous because they play well. They are famous because Mrs. Eisenberg plays the piano with only her right hand, and Mrs. Patrick plays the piano with only her left hand. They sit next to each other and play the piano together. Mrs. Eisenberg plays one part of the music, and Mrs. Patrick plays the other part.

Mrs. Eisenberg and Mrs. Patrick didn't always play the piano with only one hand. They used to play with two hands. Mrs. Patrick was a piano teacher. She taught hundreds of students. She taught her own children, too. Then, when she was 69 years old, Mrs. Patrick had a stroke. She couldn't move or speak. Gradually she got better, but her right side was still very weak. She couldn't play the piano anymore. She was very sad.

Playing the piano was Mrs. Eisenberg's hobby. She often played five or six hours a day. Then, when she was 80 years old, she, too, had a stroke. She couldn't move the left side of her body, so she couldn't play the piano anymore. She was very sad.

A few months after her stroke, Mrs. Eisenberg went to a senior citizens' center. There were a lot of activities at the center, and Mrs. Eisenberg wanted to keep busy. Mrs. Patrick wanted to keep busy, too. A few weeks later, she went to the same center. The director was showing her around the center when Mrs. Patrick saw a piano. She looked sadly at the piano. "Is anything wrong?" the director asked. "No," Mrs. Patrick answered. "The piano brings back memories. Before my stroke, I played the piano." The director looked at Mrs. Patrick's weak right hand and said, "Wait here. I'll be right back." A few minutes later the director came back with Mrs. Eisenberg. "Margaret Patrick," the director said. "Meet Ruth Eisenberg. Before her stroke, she played the piano, too. She has a good right hand, and you have a good left hand. I think you two can do something wonderful together."

"Do you know Chopin's Waltz in D flat?" Mrs. Eisenberg asked Mrs. Patrick. "Yes," Mrs. Patrick answered. The two women sat down at the piano and began to play. Mrs. Eisenberg used only her right hand, and Mrs. Patrick used only her left hand. The music sounded good. The women discovered that they loved the same music. Together they began to play the music they loved. They were not sad anymore.

Mrs. Patrick said, "Sometimes God closes a door and then opens a window. I lost my music, but I found Ruth. Now I have my music again. I have my friend Ruth, too."

2. VOCABULARY

Which words have the same meaning as the words in the story? Circle the letter of the correct answer.

1. Mrs. Patrick had a *stroke.* She couldn't move or speak.

a. a serious sickness
b. an idea

2. She got better, but her right side was still *weak.* She couldn't play the piano anymore.

a. cold
b. not strong

3. Playing the piano was Mrs. Eisenberg's *hobby.*

a. something she did for money
b. something she did in her free time

4. Mrs. Patrick and Mrs. Eisenberg *give concerts.*

a. speak, and people take pictures of them
b. play the piano, and people listen to them

3. COMPREHENSION

UNDERSTANDING CONNECTIONS

Find the best way to complete each sentence. Write the letter of your answer on the line.

1. Mrs. Eisenberg plays the piano with her right hand, and ______

2. Mrs. Eisenberg plays one part of the music, and ______

3. Mrs. Patrick was a piano teacher, and ______

4. Mrs. Patrick was 69 years old when she had a stroke, and ______

5. Mrs. Patrick says that sometimes God closes a door, and ______

a. Mrs. Eisenberg played the piano as a hobby.

b. Mrs. Patrick plays only with her left hand.

c. then God opens a window.

d. Mrs. Patrick plays the other part.

e. Mrs. Eisenberg was 80.

MAKING INFERENCES

Find the best way to complete each sentence. Write the letter of your answer on the line. (The answers are not in the story; you have to guess.)

1. Mrs. Eisenberg and Mrs. Patrick give concerts in the United States and in Canada, so probably __b__

2. Mrs. Patrick taught the piano to hundreds of students, so probably ______

3. Mrs. Patrick and Mrs. Eisenberg went to the same senior citizens' center, so probably ______

4. Both women knew Chopin's Waltz in D flat, so probably ______

a. they live in the same city.

b. they travel often.

c. they like classical music.

d. she was a piano teacher for many years.

UNDERSTANDING A SUMMARY

Imagine this: You want to tell the story "Margaret Patrick . . . Meet Ruth Eisenberg" to a friend. You want to tell the story quickly, in only six sentences. Which six sentences tell the story best? Check (✔) your answer.

1. ____ Two women played the piano. One woman was a piano teacher; she taught hundreds of students and her own children, too. The other woman played the piano as a hobby; she often played five or six hours a day. Both women had strokes and couldn't play the piano anymore. They were very sad. The women wanted to keep busy, so they went to a senior citizens' center

2. ____ Two women had strokes and couldn't play the piano anymore. One woman couldn't use her left arm, and the other woman couldn't use her right arm. One day the women met at a senior citizens' center. They discovered they could play the piano together. Now they give concerts. One woman plays one part of the music with her left hand, and the other woman plays the other part with her right hand.

4. DISCUSSION

Mrs. Patrick and Mrs. Eisenberg had a lot in common: They both played the piano, they loved the same music, and they both had strokes. What about you and your partner? Do you have anything in common? Find out.

Read the sentences below and check (✔) the sentences that are true for you.

1. ___ I play the piano.
2. ___ I like to travel.
3. ___ I like rock music.
4. ___ I tell good jokes.
5. ___ I like to swim.
6. ___ I like to dance.
7. ___ I like Chinese food.
8. ___ I have a dog.
9. ___ I have a cat.
10. ___ I like to walk.
11. ___ I watch a lot of TV.
12. ___ I think English is difficult.
13. ___ I have a vegetable garden.
14. ___ I like to use computers.
15. ___ I play soccer.
16. ___ I like to shop.
17. ___ I like to drive fast.
18. ✔ ______________________ (Add your own sentence.)
19. ✔ ______________________ (Add your own sentence.)
20. ✔ ______________________ (Add your own sentence.)

Read the sentences you checked to your partner. Did you and your partner check any of the same sentences? What do you have in common?

5. WRITING

What do you and your partner have in common? Make a list. For example:

We both like to walk.
We both play the piano.

Now write your sentences on your own paper.

UNIT 12

1. PRE-READING

Look at the pictures.

- What is the woman doing in the first picture?
- What happened to the woman in the second picture?

Read the title of the story. Look at the pictures again.

- What do you think this story is about?
- Can you guess what happened?

The Bed

Is it difficult for you to get up in the morning? Do you sometimes oversleep? Are you often late for work or school? Yes? Then Hiroyuki Sugiyama of Japan has a special bed for you. Hiroyuki's bed will get you up in the morning! Here is how it works.

The bed is connected to an alarm clock. First, the alarm clock rings. You have a few minutes to wake up. Next, a tape recorder in the bed plays soft music or other pleasant sounds. The tape recorder in Hiroyuki's bed plays a recording of his girlfriend. She whispers in a sweet voice, "Wake up, darling, please." A few minutes later a second recording plays. The second recording can be loud music or unpleasant sounds. Hiroyuki hears a recording of his boss. His boss shouts, "Wake up immediately, or you'll be late!"

If you don't get up after the second recording, you'll be sorry. A mechanical "foot" is in the bed. The mechanical foot kicks you in the head. Then the bed waits a few more minutes. What! You're still in bed! Slowly the top of the bed rises higher and higher. The foot of the bed goes lower and lower. Finally, the bed is vertical. You slide off the bed and onto the floor. You are out of bed and awake!

The woman in the pictures is demonstrating Hiroyuki's bed. In the first picture, the bed is rising a little. The woman is still sleeping. In the second picture, the bed is almost vertical. The woman is not sleeping anymore.

Hiroyuki made his bed because he wanted to win a contest. He works for Honda Motor Company. Once every two years Honda has a contest—the "All-Honda Idea Contest." It is for Honda's 200,000 employees. The employees think of new ideas. If their ideas win, the employees win prizes. Hiroyuki Sugiyama won one of the top prizes for his bed.

Hiroyuki wanted to win a prize. He also wanted to solve a problem. "Getting up in the morning is difficult for me," Hiroyuki said. "Often I am almost late for work. Maybe this bed will solve my problem."

Hiroyuki's bed is not in stores. There is only one bed—the bed Hiroyuki made for the contest. Maybe someday a company will make Hiroyuki's bed and sell it in stores. Maybe people will buy millions of beds. Then Hiroyuki will be rich. If the bed makes Hiroyuki rich, it certainly will solve his problem. Hiroyuki will have a lot of money. He won't need to go to work, and he won't need to get up early!

2. VOCABULARY

Read the sentences. Guess the meaning of the words. Circle the letter of your answer.

1. The tape recorder plays soft music or other *pleasant* sounds.

a. nice
b. fast

2. His girlfriend *whispers* in a sweet voice, "Wake up, darling, please."

a. speaks very quietly
b. speaks very loudly

3. The top of the bed rises higher and higher. The foot of the bed goes lower and lower. Finally, the bed is *vertical.* Which line is vertical?

a. ———— **b.** |

4. The woman in the picture is *demonstrating* the bed.

a. making
b. showing

3. COMPREHENSION

FINDING INFORMATION

Read the questions. Find the answers in the story. Write the answers.

1. Did Hiroyuki make a special bed or a special car?
   He made a special bed.
2. Is the bed for people who can't sleep or for people who oversleep?
   ____
3. Is the bed connected to an alarm clock or to a TV?
   ____
4. Does the bed have a telephone or a tape recorder?
   ____
5. Does Hiroyuki work for Honda Motor Company or for Ford Motor Company?
   ____
6. Did Hiroyuki make the bed because he wanted to win a contest or because he works in a bed factory?
   ____

REMEMBERING DETAILS

Hiroyuki is sleeping in his bed. He doesn't get up. What will happen to him? Check (✔) six answers.

____ An alarm clock will ring.

____ A tape recorder will play a recording of his girlfriend.

____ The tape recorder will play a recording of his boss.

____ The bed will shake.

____ The bed will take Hiroyuki's pillow and blanket.

____ Hiroyuki will slide onto the floor.

____ A mechanical foot will kick Hiroyuki in the head.

____ The bed will rise higher and higher.

UNDERSTANDING CAUSE AND EFFECT

Find the best way to complete each sentence. Write the letter of your answer on the line.

1. Getting up in the morning is a problem for Hiroyuki, so ____

2. Hiroyuki won the contest, so ____

3. Finally, the bed is vertical, so ____

4. The bed is not in stores, so ____

a. he got a prize.

b. the sleeper slides off the bed and onto the floor.

c. he is often almost late for work.

d. you can't buy it.

4. DISCUSSION

Interview a partner. Ask your partner the following questions and listen carefully. Write your partner's answers on your own paper. When you are finished, sit in groups of four. Tell the other students in your group what you learned about your partner.

1. Is getting up in the morning easy or difficult for you?
2. Would you like to have Hiroyuki's bed?
3. When do you usually go to bed?
4. When do you usually get up?
5. Is getting up in the morning difficult for anybody in your family? Who is it? How do you get him or her out of bed?
6. Do people in your native country sleep in the afternoon? How long do they sleep?
7. Do you like to sleep in the afternoon? How long do you sleep?
8. Hiroyuki is often almost late for work. Are you often late, or are you always on time?

5. WRITING

Hiroyuki made a new bed. The bed was Hiroyuki's invention. Do you have an idea for an invention?

Draw a picture of your invention. Give your invention a name. What does your invention do? Write about it. Here is an example.

If you put on these glasses, you will know your partner's feelings.

UNIT 13

1. PRE-READING

Look at the picture.

- What language is on the postage stamp?
- What year is on the stamp?

Read the title of the story. Look at the picture again.

- Who was Mr. Andropov?
- What kind of writing begins "Dear . . ."?
- What do you think this story is about?
- Can you guess what happens?

Dear Mr. Andropov

Samantha Smith, a little girl from Maine, was frightened. On TV she saw programs about nuclear bombs. In news magazines she saw pictures of missiles. It was 1983. The United States and the Soviet Union were enemies, and the two countries were ready for war.

Samantha decided to write a letter to Yuri Andropov, who was the leader of the Soviet Union. She wrote:

Dear Mr. Andropov,

My name is Samantha Smith. I am ten years old. I am worried about nuclear war. How are you going to help so we don't have a war? Please tell me.

I have another question, but you don't have to answer it. Why do you want to conquer the world or at least our country? God wants us to live together in peace and not to fight.

Sincerely,
Samantha Smith

A few months later, Samantha received a letter from Mr. Andropov. The letter said: "The Soviet Union doesn't want war with the United States. We want peace and friendship. Please visit my country. I want you to learn about the Soviet Union and to meet Soviet children. Summer is the best time to visit."

Samantha and her parents decided to accept Mr. Andropov's invitation. In the summer, they flew to the Soviet Union. First they went to Russia, which was then part of the Soviet Union. Guides took them to important and beautiful places. Samantha learned to sing Russian songs and dance Russian dances. Sometimes she wore traditional Russian clothes.

People in both the Soviet Union and the United States watched Samantha on TV. Samantha won their hearts. She was friendly and cheerful, a beautiful child with a big smile. Everyone liked her.

At a children's camp in the Soviet Union, Samantha became friends with Natasha, a Soviet girl. Natasha and Samantha swam together and played the piano together. They talked about music and clothes. "Natasha and I are friends," Samantha thought. "Why can't our countries be friends?"

Later Samantha wrote a book about her trip. On the first page she wrote, "I dedicate this book to the children of the world. They know that peace is always possible."

Two years after her trip, Samantha Smith died in a plane crash. She was thirteen years old.

The Soviet people didn't want to forget Samantha. They put her picture on a postage stamp. They named a mountain, a flower, and a ship "Samantha Smith." When a Soviet astronomer discovered a new planet, he named it "Samantha Smith." The astronomer said, "Samantha lived a short life. But she shone very brightly in it."

2. VOCABULARY

Complete the sentences with the words below.

cheerful	frightened	astronomer	enemies

1. In 1983 the United States and the Soviet Union were not friends; they were ___enemies___.

2. Samantha was afraid of war. She was ________________ when she saw nuclear bombs on TV.

3. Samantha was a friendly child with a big smile. Everyone liked her because she was ________________.

4. A Soviet scientist discovered a new planet in the sky. The ________________ named the planet "Samantha Smith."

3. COMPREHENSION

FINDING INFORMATION

What information is in the story? What information is not in the story?

There are two correct ways to complete each sentence. Circle the letters of the *two* correct answers.

1. Samantha Smith
 (**a.**) was ten years old.
 b. was a good student in school.
 (**c.**) was from Maine.

2. Samantha was frightened because she saw
 a. programs about nuclear bombs on TV.
 b. pictures of missiles in news magazines.
 c. war movies on TV.

3. In her letter to Mr. Andropov, Samantha wrote:
 a. "I want to visit the Soviet Union."
 b. "I am worried about war."
 c. "Why do you want to conquer the world?"

4. In his letter, Mr. Andropov wrote:
 a. "We don't want war with the United States."
 b. "Please visit my country."
 c. "Don't believe everything you see on TV."

5. In Russia, Samantha
 a. learned to sing Russian songs.
 b. taught English to Russian children.
 c. wore traditional Russian clothes.

6. The Soviet people didn't want to forget Samantha, so they
 a. put her picture on a postage stamp.
 b. named a mountain "Samantha Smith."
 c. wrote a book about her.

UNDERSTANDING REASONS

Find the best way to complete each sentence. Write the letter of your answer on the line.

1. Samantha wrote Mr. Andropov ____
2. Mr. Andropov wrote Samantha ____
3. People in both the United States and the Soviet Union turned on their TVs ____
4. Samantha went to a children's camp ____
5. The Soviet people put Samantha's picture on a postage stamp ____

a. to remember her.
b. to watch Samantha.
c. to meet Soviet children.
d. to invite her to visit the Soviet Union.
e. to ask him some questions.

REVIEWING THE STORY

Complete each sentence. Then read the story again and check your answers.

Samantha Smith wrote a ___letter___(1) to Yuri Andropov. She wrote, "I am worried ___________(2) nuclear war. How are you going to help so we don't have a ___________(3)?" Mr. Andropov invited Samantha and her parents to ___________(4) his country. In July 1983 they went to the ___________(5) Union. Samantha became friends with Natasha, a Soviet ___________(6). Samantha thought, "We are friends. Why can't our ___________(7) be friends?"

Samantha wrote a ___________(8) about her trip to the Soviet Union. On the first page she wrote, "I dedicate this book to the ___________(9) of the world. They know that ___________(10) is always possible."

4. DISCUSSION

Soviet guides took Samantha to important and beautiful places. Imagine that a classmate is going to visit your country. You will be your classmate's guide. You will take your classmate to important and beautiful places.

Draw a map of your country. Put the places that you will visit on the map. Show the map to your classmate. Tell your classmate about each place on the map.

5. WRITING

A. Samantha learned that American girls and Soviet girls are alike in many ways. In what ways are Americans and people from your native country alike? In what ways are they different?

On your own paper, make two lists with these headings:

Americans and people from my country are alike. For example:	*Americans and people from my country are different. For example:*

B. Write a letter to the leader of a country. Tell the leader your opinions.

UNIT 14

1. PRE-READING

Look at the picture.

- Where are these people?
- How do you think the man feels?
- How do you think the boy feels?

Read the title of the story. Look at the picture again.

- Who do you think the man is?
- What do you think this story is about?
- Can you guess what happens?

Parents at School

Tom, a 13-year-old boy, was a student at a junior high school in Ohio. He was not a good student. He did not behave at school. He talked in class, and he was often late. His teachers told him, "Go to the principal's office."

John Lazares was the principal at Tom's school. Tom went to Mr. Lazares's office. First Mr. Lazares disciplined Tom. He told him, "You have to stay at school an extra hour tomorrow." Then Mr. Lazares tried to talk to Tom, but Tom didn't pay much attention. "He'll be back in my office soon," Mr. Lazares thought. He told Tom, "If your teachers send you to my office again, I'm going to call your mother. I'm going to say, 'The teachers are having problems with your son. Please come to school. I want you to go to classes with him.'"

Suddenly Tom sat up in his chair. "Oh, no!" he said. "Don't do that! I don't want my mother at school! I'll be good. I promise."

Later Mr. Lazares thought about Tom's words: "I don't want my mother at school." "Hmm," Mr. Lazares thought. "Maybe I have a new way to discipline students."

In the United States, principals and teachers discipline students in several ways. The teacher often writes or calls the student's parents. Sometimes students have to stay at school for an extra hour. If a student behaves very badly, the principal can suspend the student. The student cannot come to school for one, two, or three days. Mr. Lazares didn't like to suspend students. When he suspended some students, they were happy. "A three-day vacation!" they thought.

A few days later, another boy was in Mr. Lazares's office. The boy was not behaving in class. Mr. Lazares telephoned the boy's parents. "If you come to school with your son, I won't suspend him," he said. The boy's father came to school and went with his son to every class. Other students stared at the boy and his father. The boy was embarrassed. After that, he behaved better. He didn't want his father to come to school again. Other students behaved better, too. They thought, "I don't want *my* parents to come to school!"

That year about 60 parents came to school with children who didn't behave. The next year only a few parents had to come to school. The students were behaving better.

Principals at other schools heard about Mr. Lazares's new way to discipline students. Now principals all over the United States are trying Mr. Lazares's idea. They, too, think that students behave better when parents come to school.

2. VOCABULARY

Complete the sentences. Find the right words. Circle the letter of your answer.

1. Tom talked in class and he was often late. He did not ____ at school.

a. read
b. behave
c. write

2. The principal told Tom, "You have to stay at school an extra hour tomorrow." The principal ____ him.

a. helped
b. saw
c. disciplined

3. Students who behave very badly cannot come to school for one, two, or three days. The principal ____ them.

a. visits
b. suspends
c. telephones

4. Other students stared at the boy and his father. The boy was ____.

a. injured
b. surprised
c. embarrassed

3. COMPREHENSION

UNDERSTANDING THE MAIN IDEA

Circle the letter of the best answer.

1. Another good title for this story is
- **a.** "The Boy Who Didn't Behave."
- **b.** "A New Way to Discipline Students."
- **c.** "Junior High Schools in the United States."

2. Students at Mr. Lazares's junior high school are behaving better because
- **a.** they are afraid of the teachers.
- **b.** Mr. Lazares suspends students who don't behave.
- **c.** they don't want their parents at school.

UNDERSTANDING CAUSE AND EFFECT

Find the best way to complete each sentence. Write the letter of your answer on the line.

1. Tom didn't behave at school, so ____

2. Tom didn't want his mother at school, so ____

3. Some students want a three-day vacation, so ____

4. Other students stared at the boy and his father, so ____

5. The other students didn't want their parents to come to school, so ____

a. he said, "I'll be good. I promise."

b. the boy was embarrassed.

c. his teachers sent him to the principal's office.

d. they behaved better.

e. they are happy when the principal suspends them.

UNDERSTANDING A SUMMARY

Imagine this: You want to tell the story "Parents at School" to a friend. You want to tell the story quickly, in only four sentences. Which four sentences tell the story best? Check (✔) your answer.

1. ____ The principal of a junior high school in Ohio has a new way to discipline students. If students don't behave, their parents have to come to school with them. Students at the school are behaving better now. Principals all over the United States are trying this new way to discipline students.

2. ____ Tom, a 13-year-old boy, is a student at a junior high school in Ohio. Tom didn't behave well at school: He talked in class, and he was often late. The teachers often sent Tom to the principal's office. The principal tried to talk to Tom, but Tom didn't pay much attention.

4. DISCUSSION

Joe

Pete

Joe and Pete are students. Joe is a good student; Pete isn't. What does Joe do?

With your classmates, make a list of the things that Joe does. Then make a list of the things that Pete does. For example:

Joe	*Pete*
He always does his homework.	*He is always late.*

What kind of student were you—a student like Joe or a student like Pete? Tell your classmates.

5. WRITING

Interview a partner. Ask your partner these questions about his or her elementary school. Listen carefully to your partner's answers and take notes.

1. How many children were in a class at your school?
2. Was the teacher strict or not strict?
3. How did the teacher discipline students who didn't behave well?
4. Did you behave well at school?

You can write a paragraph from your partner's answers. Here is what one student wrote.

When Pedro went to school, there were about 50 children in a class. The teacher was very strict. When the students didn't behave, they had to stand in a corner of the classroom. Sometimes the teacher hit the students' hands with a ruler. Pedro was afraid of the teacher, so he behaved very well.

Now write your paragraph on your own paper.

UNIT 15

1. PRE-READING

Look at the picture.

- Where is this?
- What do you think the people are doing?

Read the title of the story. Look at the picture again.

- What does the expression "Finders Keepers" mean?
- What do you think this story is about?
- Can you guess what happens?

Finders Keepers?

Mel Kiser was driving along a busy highway in Columbus, Ohio. He saw an armored truck a few cars ahead of him. Suddenly the back doors of the armored truck opened, and a blue plastic bag fell out of the truck. A car in front of Mr. Kiser hit the bag. The bag ripped, and money spilled out. Then another bag fell out of the truck, and another. Money was flying everywhere.

At first, drivers thought the green papers on the highway were leaves. Then they realized that the green papers were not leaves—they were money! Drivers slammed on their brakes and stopped right in the middle of the highway. People jumped out of their cars and began picking up money. They were putting ten-, twenty-, and one-hundred-dollar bills into their pockets. One man was yelling, "Money, money, money! It's all free! Grab some while you can!"

Mr. Kiser also got out of his car. He grabbed a plastic bag of money, put the bag in his car, and drove away.

Later Mr. Kiser counted the money. He had $57,000. For the next two hours Mr. Kiser thought about the money. He dreamed about spending it. He needed a new furnace for his house. He wanted to take a vacation in Florida. But he decided to return the money. He drove to the police station and gave the police the $57,000.

Mr. Kiser returned $57,000, and other people returned money, too. But over one million dollars were still missing. The armored truck company offered a 10 percent reward. "If you return $1,000, for example, we will pay you $100," the company said. Mel Kiser had returned $57,000, so the company gave him a reward of $5,700. A few more people returned money and got rewards, but most of the money—almost a million dollars—was still missing.

Then the armored truck company got some help. A man telephoned and said, "I was driving along the highway when I saw a traffic jam ahead. I didn't want to be in the traffic jam, so I took the next exit and got off the highway. Then I saw the money. People were running everywhere. I had a camera in my car and I took some pictures. Would you like the pictures?"

"Yes!" answered the armored truck company. The company gave the pictures to the police. The police looked closely at the pictures. They looked at the cars, the license plates, and the people's faces. They tried to find the people who had taken the money, but they didn't have much luck.

One man who had taken money telephoned a Columbus newspaper. The man did not give his name. "I took two bags of money," he said. "I'm going to take the money and leave Columbus. I have enough money for the rest of my life."

2. VOCABULARY

Complete the sentences with the words below.

grabbing	armored truck	ripped	slammed on their brakes

1. The truck ahead of Mel Kiser was small and strong, and it carried money. It was an *armored truck*.
2. When cars hit the plastic bags, the bags broke and opened. The bags ______________.
3. The drivers stopped suddenly. They ______________.
4. People were running everywhere and taking money. They were ______________ ten-, twenty-, and one-hundred-dollar bills.

3. COMPREHENSION

REMEMBERING DETAILS

Read the sentences. One word in each sentence is not correct. Find the word and cross it out. Write the correct word.

1. Mel Kiser was driving along a ~~quiet~~ *busy* highway in Columbus, Ohio.
2. He saw an armored bus a few cars ahead of him.
3. Suddenly the back doors of the armored truck closed.
4. A blue paper bag fell out of the truck.
5. The bag ripped, and leaves spilled out.
6. People jumped out of their houses and began picking up money.
7. They were putting ten-, thirty-, and one-hundred-dollar bills into their pockets.
8. The armored truck company offered a 10 percent tax.
9. More people returned money, but almost a million pennies were still missing.

UNDERSTANDING TIME RELATIONSHIPS

Find the best way to complete each sentence. Write the letter of your answer on the line.

1. When the back doors of the armored truck opened, ____
2. When cars hit the plastic bags, ____
3. When drivers realized that the green papers were money, ____
4. When Mr. Kiser went to the police station, ____
5. When the armored truck company offered a reward, ____

a. they slammed on their brakes.
b. the bags ripped.
c. blue plastic bags fell out of the truck.
d. more people returned money.
e. he returned $57,000.

MAKING INFERENCES

Find the best way to complete each sentence. Write the letter of your answer on the line. (The answers are not in the story; you have to guess.)

1. There is a busy highway in Columbus, Ohio, so probably ____

2. The driver of the armored truck didn't stop, so probably ____

3. Mel Kiser needed a furnace, so probably ____

4. Mel Kiser returned all the money, so probably ____

5. One man said, "I have enough money for the rest of my life," so probably ____

a. he didn't realize that money was falling from the truck.

b. Columbus is a big city.

c. he found a lot of money.

d. he is an honest man.

e. the weather is sometimes cold in Ohio.

4. DISCUSSION

Imagine this: You are walking in a big city in your native country. You find a bag on the sidewalk. There is $57,000 in the bag.

What will you do with the money? Check (✔) one answer.

____ I will keep the money.

____ I will give the money to the police. I will tell the police, "Try to find the owner of the money."

____ I will try to find the owner of the money myself.

____ I will give the money to poor people.

____ ____

(Write your own answer.)

Explain your answer in a small group.

5. WRITING

Imagine that you see bags of money on a highway. What will you do? Complete the story on your own paper.

Last week I was driving along a busy highway when I saw an armored truck a few cars ahead of me. Suddenly the back doors of the truck opened, and a blue plastic bag fell out of the truck. A car in front of me hit the bag. The bag ripped, and money spilled out. Then another bag fell out of the truck, and another. Money was flying everywhere. I . . .

UNIT 16

1 PRE-READING

Look at the picture.

- Why do you think the girl has no hair?
- How do you think she feels?
- What is she holding?

Read the title of the story. Look at the picture again.

- What is an auction?
- Can you guess what happens?

The Auction

Katie Fisher was excited. It was July 15—the day of the animal auction. "Today I'm going to sell my lamb," she thought.

Seventeen-year-old Katie lived on a farm in Madison County, Ohio. Every July there was an animal auction in Madison County. Children from farms all over the county brought their best animals to an arena. They sold their animals to the farmer who paid the highest price. "I hope I get a good price for my lamb," Katie thought.

On the afternoon of the auction, Katie walked into the center of the arena with her lamb. People were a little surprised when they saw Katie. She had no hair. She had no hair because of chemotherapy. Katie had cancer. The chemotherapy had stopped the cancer, and Katie felt much better. But Katie's parents had a lot of medical bills to pay. Katie wanted to sell her lamb and pay some of her medical bills.

The auctioneer decided to say a few words about Katie. "This young lady needs money for her medical bills," the auctioneer said. "Let's give her a good price for her lamb." Then the auctioneer began the auction.

"Who'll give me one dollar a pound for this lamb?" he began.

"One dollar!" a farmer said.

"I hear one dollar," the auctioneer said. "Who'll give me two dollars a pound?"

"Two dollars!" another farmer said.

"I hear two dollars," the auctioneer continued. "Who'll give me three dollars?"

The auctioneer continued to raise the price of the lamb, and the farmers continued to offer more money. Finally, Katie's lamb sold for twelve dollars a pound.

Katie was happy. Lambs usually sold for two dollars a pound, but her lamb sold for twelve dollars a pound! She took her lamb to the farmer who bought it. The farmer paid Katie for the lamb and then said something surprising: "Keep the lamb," he told Katie. "Sell it again."

Katie walked back into the center of the arena with her lamb. Smiling, the auctioneer said, "Well, I guess I have to sell this lamb again." A second farmer bought the lamb, this time for eight dollars a pound.

When the auctioneer sold the lamb for the second time, something amazing happened. The farm families in the arena began chanting, "Sell it again! Sell it again!" When Katie took her lamb to the second farmer, he paid her for the lamb. Then he smiled and said, "You heard the people. Keep the lamb. Sell it again."

Katie walked back into the center of the arena with her lamb, and the crowd cheered. The auctioneer sold Katie's lamb again . . . and again . . . and again. Every time the auctioneer sold the lamb, the crowd chanted, "Sell it again! Sell it again!"

That afternoon the farmers of Madison County, Ohio, bought Katie's lamb 36 times. All 36 farmers paid Katie, but not one farmer took the lamb. Katie went home with $16,000—enough money to pay all her medical bills. She also went home with her lamb.

2. VOCABULARY

Complete the sentences with the words below.

cheered	chanted	crowd	auctioneer

1. Hundreds of farm families went to the animal auction. There was a big ____crowd____ of people.
2. Before he began the auction, the ____________ said a few words about Katie.
3. The farm families repeated the same words. "Sell it again! Sell it again!" they ____________.
4. The people at the arena were happy when Katie walked back into the center of the arena with her lamb, so they ____________.

3. COMPREHENSION

REMEMBERING DETAILS

One word in each sentence is not correct. Find the word and cross it out. Write the correct word.

1. Katie Fisher was excited because she was going to sell her ~~cow~~. *lamb*
2. Seven-year-old Katie lived on a farm in Madison County, Ohio.
3. Every December there was an animal auction in Madison County.
4. Children from farms all over the world brought their best animals to an arena.
5. They sold their animals to the farmer who paid the lowest price.
6. Lambs usually sold for two cents a pound, but Katie's lamb sold for twelve dollars a pound.
7. Katie took her lamb to the auctioneer who bought it.
8. The farmer thanked Katie for the lamb and then said, "Keep the lamb."

UNDERSTANDING CAUSE AND EFFECT

Find the best way to complete each sentence. Write the letter of your answer on the line.

1. Katie wanted to sell her lamb ____
2. The people in the arena were surprised when they saw Katie ____
3. The second farmer who bought the lamb told Katie, "You heard the people" ____
4. Katie got $16,000 for her lamb ____
5. Katie went home with her lamb ____

a. because the farm families were chanting, "Sell it again."

b. because the farmers bought it 36 times.

c. because the farmers who bought the lamb didn't take it.

d. because she had no hair.

e. because she needed money for medical bills.

UNDERSTANDING A SUMMARY

Imagine this: You want to tell the story "The Auction" to a friend. You want to tell the story quickly, in only four sentences. Which four sentences tell the story best? Check (✔) your answer.

1. ____ A seventeen-year-old girl who had cancer needed money for her medical bills. She decided to sell her lamb at an auction in Madison County, Ohio. The auction happens every July in Madison County. Farm children take their best animals to an arena and sell them to the farmer who pays the highest price.

2. ____ A seventeen-year-old girl who had cancer needed money for her medical bills. She decided to sell her lamb at an auction. Every time she sold her lamb, the farmer who bought it didn't take it. She sold the lamb 36 times and went home with $16,000—enough money to pay all her medical bills.

4. DISCUSSION

The farm families did something kind for Katie. People do kind things every day. For example: They give money to poor people; they help people who are lost; they open doors for people who are carrying packages.

Did someone do something kind for you? Did *you* do something kind for someone? In a small group, tell your classmates about it.

5. WRITING

Katie Fisher keeps a diary. Every night, she writes down what happened that day. What did Katie write on the night of July 15?

On your own paper, finish the page in Katie's diary.

July 15

This afternoon I went to the arena to sell my lamb. I walked into the center of the arena. The auctioneer told the people I needed money for medical bills. Then he began the auction. The lamb sold for twelve dollars a pound! I took my lamb to the farmer who bought it. He . . .

UNIT 17

1. PRE-READING

Look at the picture.

- How do you think this woman feels?
- What is the woman doing with the money?
- Why do you think she is doing that?

Read the title of the story. Look at the picture again.

- What do you think this story is about?
- Can you guess what happens?

Money to Burn

Lillian Beard whistled and smiled while she worked. "Why are you so happy?" her co-workers asked her.

"Last week I got my income tax refund," Lillian answered. "This morning I went to the bank and cashed the check. I have $462 in my pocket. I'm thinking about the money. How will I spend it?"

After work Lillian came home and decided to wash some clothes. She looked at the jeans she was wearing. They were dirty, so she put them in the washing machine, too. Ten minutes later she remembered: "The money! It's still in the pocket of my jeans!" Lillian ran to the washing machine and took out the jeans. The money was still in the pocket, but it was wet. Lillian put the money on the kitchen table to dry.

A few hours later the money was still wet. "Hmm," Lillian thought. "How can I dry this money?" Then Lillian had an idea. She could dry the money in her microwave oven! Lillian put the money in the microwave, set the timer for five minutes, and left the kitchen.

When Lillian came back a few minutes later, she saw a fire in the microwave. She opened the oven door, blew out the fire, and looked at her money. The money was burned.

The next day Lillian took the burned money to the bank. A teller at the bank told her, "If I can see the numbers on the burned bills, I can give you new money." Unfortunately, the teller found numbers on only a few bills. The teller took those bills and gave Lillian $17.

A newspaper reporter heard about the burned money. He wrote a story about Lillian for the newspaper. Several people read the story and called the newspaper. "Tell Ms. Beard to send the burned money to the U.S. Department of Treasury," the people said. "Maybe she can get her money back."

Every year about 30,000 people send damaged money to the Treasury Department. Experts there look carefully at the damaged money. Sometimes they can give people new money for the damaged money. Once a farmer dropped his wallet in a field, and a cow ate his money—thousands of dollars. The farmer killed the cow and sent the cow's stomach, with the money inside, to the Treasury Department. The experts gave the farmer new money.

Lillian sent her money to the Treasury Department. The experts looked at Lillian's burned money and sent her a check for $231. What did Lillian buy with the money? She didn't buy anything. She gave the $231 to friends who needed money. Lillian said, "When I burned the $462, I thought, 'Well, my money is gone.' The check for $231 was a big surprise. I decided to give the money to my friends. Money is important, but people are more important to me."

2. VOCABULARY

Complete the sentences with the words below.

set the timer	income	refund	experts

1. Lillian works and earns money. She pays tax on the money she earns. She pays ___income___ tax.
2. When Lillian paid her income tax, she gave the government too much money. The government gave her some money back. Lillian got a ______________ on her income tax.
3. Lillian wanted the microwave oven to heat the money for five minutes, so she ______________ for five minutes.
4. People at the Treasury Department know a lot about money. They are ______________.

3. COMPREHENSION

REMEMBERING DETAILS

What did Lillian Beard do with her money? Check (✔) seven answers.

__ She put it in her pocket.
__ She washed it with her jeans.
__ She put it on the kitchen table to dry.
__ She counted it many times.
__ She burned it in her microwave oven.
__ She showed it to a teller at the bank.
__ She sent it to the Treasury Department.
__ She spent it.
__ She gave it to friends.

UNDERSTANDING PRONOUNS

Look at the pronouns. What do they mean? Write the letter of your answer on the line.

1. ____ Lillian cashed *it.*
2. ____ Lillian decided to wash *them.*
3. ____ *It* was damaged.
4. ____ Lillian set *it* for five minutes.
5. ____ *He* wrote a story about Lillian.
6. ____ *It* ate a farmer's money.
7. ____ *They* looked carefully at Lillian's burned money.
8. ____ Lillian gave *them* money.

a. experts at the Treasury Department
b. her income tax refund check
c. her jeans
d. the timer
e. a newspaper reporter
f. a cow
g. friends
h. Lillian's money

UNDERSTANDING A SUMMARY

Imagine this: You want to tell the story "Money to Burn" to a friend. You want to tell the story quickly, in only four sentences. Which four sentences tell the story best? Check (✔) your answer.

1. ____ A woman who got a $462 income tax refund went to the bank and cashed the check. At work she was very happy because she had $462 in her pocket. After work she went home and washed her jeans. She forgot to take the money out of the pocket, so the money got wet.

2. ____ When a woman washed her jeans, she forgot that she had $462 in the pocket. She tried to dry the wet money in her microwave oven but burned it. She sent the burned money to experts at the U.S. Treasury Department, who mailed the woman a check for $231. The woman gave the money to her friends.

4. DISCUSSION

Lillian Beard paid tax on her income. What is taxed in your native country?

First, fill in the chart for yourself. Then ask a partner about taxes in his or her native country. Write your partner's answers on the chart.

NAME	COUNTRY	WHAT IS TAXED?	WHAT IS *NOT* TAXED?
Lillian Beard	*U.S.A.* *(state of Indiana)*	*income* *houses and land* *food people eat in restaurants* *things people buy in stores* *tickets for movies and sporting events*	*food people buy in stores*
Your name			
Your partner's name			

Tell the class what you learned about taxes in your partner's native country.

5. WRITING

Look at a coin or bill. Then describe the money in a paragraph. Here is what one student wrote:

I have a five-dinar bill from Bahrain. It is worth about 13 American dollars. Its colors are blue and green. On one side of the bill, the language is Arabic. On the other side of the bill, the language is English. There is a drawing of the airport in al-Muharraq. If you hold the bill up to the light, you can see a drawing of an ox's head.

Now write your paragraph on your own paper.

UNIT 18

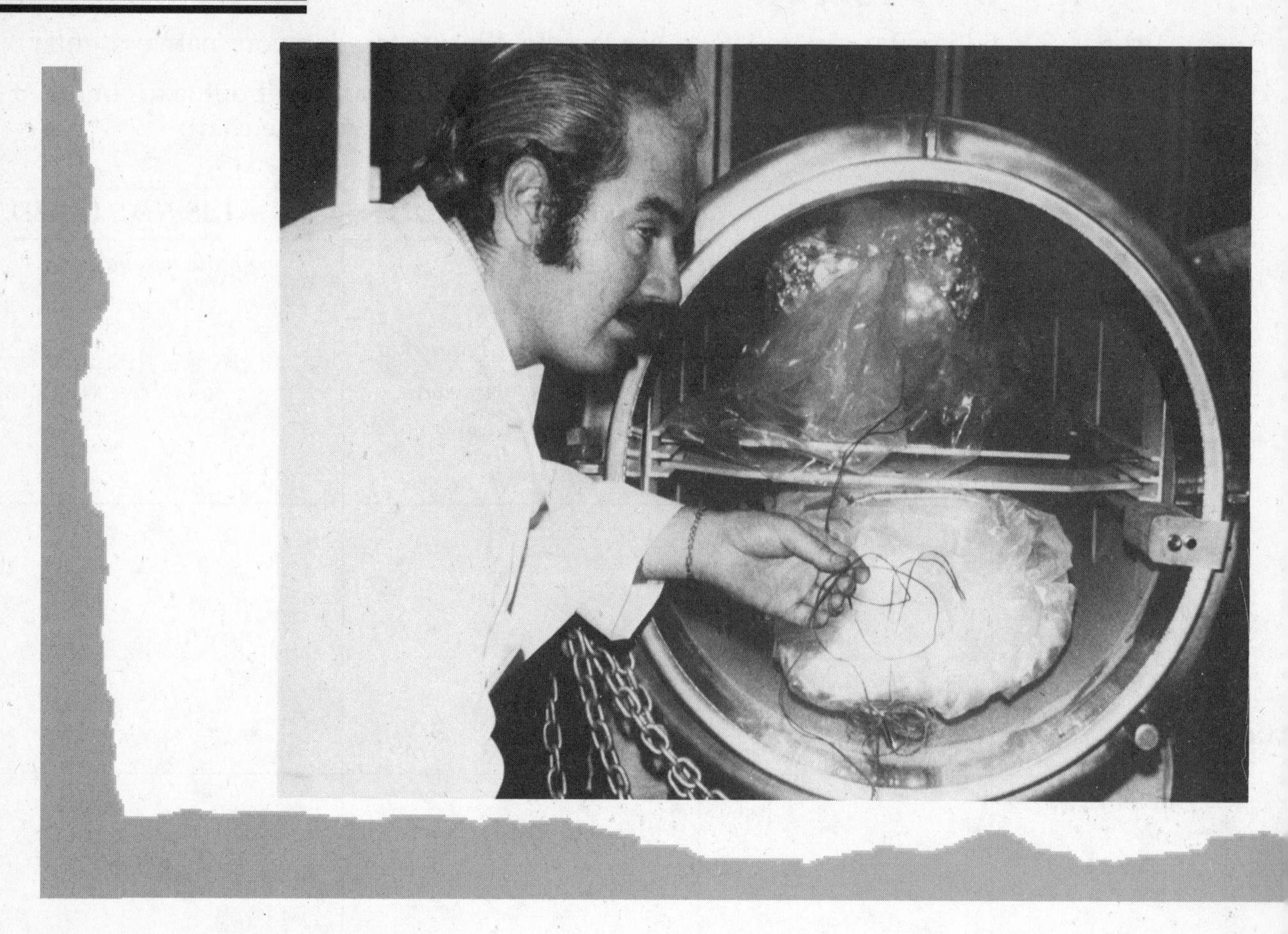

1. PRE-READING

Look at the picture.

- What kind of work do you think the man does?
- What do you see in the capsule?

Read the title of the story. Look at the picture again.

- What do you think is inside the two plastic bags in the capsule?
- What do you think this story is about?

A Chance to Live Again

The man in the picture is Art Quaife. Art Quaife is a scientist. He is also a businessman. His business is freezing people. He works for a company in California called Trans Time. Trans Time freezes people after they die.

Why does Trans Time freeze dead people? The people hope that someday they will live again. Doctors today can cure many diseases, but they cannot cure all diseases. People still get sick and die. Maybe in the future doctors will have medicine for all diseases. Some people think so. They want Trans Time to freeze their bodies after they die. Maybe 100, or 200, or 300 years later, Trans Time doctors will bring the people back to life. The doctors will cure their diseases, and the people will be alive and healthy again.

Trans Time freezes people who die of disease. They also freeze people who die of old age. Maybe someday doctors will have medicine for old age. The Trans Time doctors will bring the old people back to life and give them medicine. The old people will be young again.

People often ask the scientists at Trans Time, "How will Trans Time bring dead people back to life?" The scientists answer, "We're not sure." In 1987 a Trans Time scientist did an experiment: He froze his dog. The dog's heart stopped beating; the dog was dead. Then, 20 minutes later, the scientist brought the dog back to life. Since then, Trans Time scientists have frozen many dogs and several baboons. Trans Time scientists say, "We can freeze a healthy animal and bring it back to life. We can't freeze dead people and bring them back to life. But we think that someday it will be possible." When the scientists say "someday," they mean years from now—maybe 100 or 200 years. How can Trans Time keep people frozen for 200 years?

After a person dies, workers at Trans Time cool the body with ice and chemicals. When the body is very cold, workers put the body into a capsule. They fill the capsule with liquid nitrogen. The temperature in the capsule is –196 degrees centigrade. Every two weeks workers add more liquid nitrogen. The liquid nitrogen keeps the bodies frozen. In the picture there are two bodies in a capsule. Art Quaife is checking the temperature of the bodies.

Trans Time charges $50,000 to freeze a body and $100,000 to keep a body frozen—$150,000 all together. That is a lot of money. But some people think that $150,000 is a fair price. It's a fair price for a chance to live again.

2. VOCABULARY

Which sentences have the same meaning as the sentences in the story? Circle the letter of your answer.

1. Doctors today can *cure* many *diseases.*
   - **a.** Today doctors give sick people medicine and send them to special hospitals.
   - **b.** Today doctors give sick people medicine, and many of the sick people get well.

2. Workers *fill* the capsule with liquid nitrogen. Every two weeks they *add* more liquid nitrogen.
   - **a.** Workers put liquid nitrogen into the capsule. Two weeks later they put more liquid nitrogen into the capsule.
   - **b.** The capsules have liquid nitrogen in them. Every two weeks workers count the capsules.

3. The liquid nitrogen *keeps* the bodies frozen.
   - **a.** Trans Time does not give the bodies to other companies.
   - **b.** The bodies stay frozen in the liquid nitrogen.

4. Trans Time *charges* $50,000 to freeze a body.
   - **a.** The cost of freezing a body at Trans Time is $50,000.
   - **b.** People use credit cards when they pay Trans Time $50,000.

3. COMPREHENSION

UNDERSTANDING THE MAIN IDEA

Circle the letter of the best answer.

1. People want Trans Time to freeze their bodies because
   a. Trans Time's prices are very low.
   b. they want to live again in 100, 200, or 300 years.
   c. freezing is good for their bodies.

2. After Trans Time brings people back to life, the people will be healthy because
   a. doctors will cure their diseases.
   b. they rested a long time.
   c. freezing cures diseases.

FINDING INFORMATION

What information is in the story? What information is not in the story?

There are two correct ways to complete each sentence. Circle the letters of the *two* correct answers.

1. Trans Time freezes people who die
   a. in accidents.
   (b.) of disease.
   (c.) of old age.

2. Maybe in the future doctors will have medicine that
   a. cures all diseases.
   b. is inexpensive and easy to make.
   c. makes old people young again.

3. In 1987 a Trans Time scientist
   a. discovered a new way of freezing bodies.
   b. froze a healthy dog and stopped its heart.
   c. brought the dog back to life.

4. After a person dies, workers at Trans Time
   a. cool the body with ice and chemicals.
   b. put the body into a capsule.
   c. put some photos of the person into the capsule with the body.

5. Trans Time charges
   a. $50,000 to freeze a body.
   b. $100,000 to keep a body frozen.
   c. $1,500 for the medicine the doctors will use in the future.

MAKING INFERENCES

Find the best way to complete each sentence. Write the letter of your answer on the line. (The answers are not in the story; you have to guess.)

1. A scientist froze his own dog, so probably ____

2. Trans Time scientists use baboons in their experiments, so probably ____

3. The temperature of a capsule with liquid nitrogen is -196 degrees centigrade, so probably ____

4. Art Quaife is checking the temperature of the bodies, so probably ____

a. those animals and people have similar bodies.

b. he thought, "I am sure I can bring this animal back to life."

c. liquid nitrogen is very cold.

d. it is important to check the temperature often.

4. DISCUSSION

Read the question. Check (✓) your answer. Then explain your answer in a small group.

Do you want Trans Time to freeze your body after you die?

__ Yes

__ No

__ Maybe

5. WRITING

Imagine that Trans Time freezes you and brings you back to life in 300 years. Write three sentences about the world you will see. For example:

- *I will see people from other planets. People from earth will marry these people.*
- *Computers will do all our work.*
- *The earth will be one big country; there will be no borders.*

Now write your sentences.

1. ____________________

2. ____________________

3. ____________________

UNIT 19

1. PRE-READING

Look at the picture and the map.

- How do you think the men feel?
- What do you see in the water?
- Where is Costa Rica on the map?

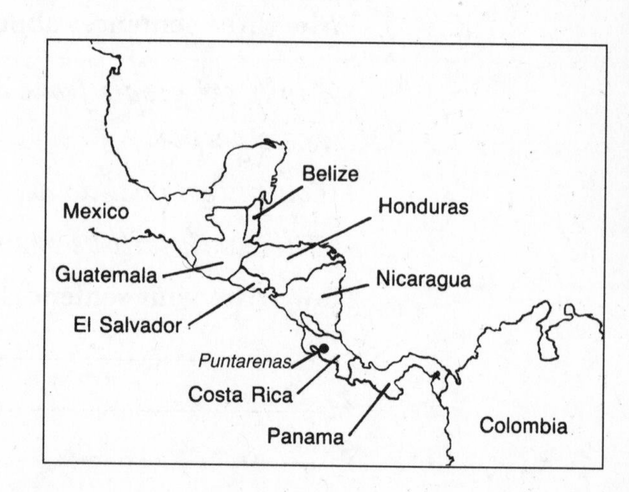

Read the title of the story. Look at the picture again.

- What kind of work do the men do?
- What do you think this story is about?
- Can you guess what happens?

A Long Fishing Trip

On a warm January morning, Joel Gonzalez kissed his wife goodbye. Joel is a fisherman, and he was going on a short fishing trip. "I'll see you in a week," he said. But Joel did not see his wife in a week. He did not see his wife again for a long, long time.

Joel left his house and went to the harbor in Puntarenas, Costa Rica. He got on a fishing boat. Four other fishermen were on the boat, too. The boat left the harbor and the men began to fish.

The first few hours on the ocean were not unusual. Then there was a terrible storm. The storm lasted for 22 days. When the storm finally stopped, the men checked their boat. Their fishing nets were gone. The engine and the radio didn't work. There was no food, and there was no fresh water.

For the next few hours, the men talked and planned. "How can we survive on the ocean?" they asked one another. Without their nets, the men couldn't fish. But they could reach out of the boat and catch big turtles. The men didn't want to eat raw turtle meat, so they needed a fire for cooking. They tore down the boat's wood cabin and made a fire with the wood.

They needed protection from the sun and rain, so they built a simple roof. The roof held rainwater, too. The men could drink rainwater from the roof.

For the next five months the men ate turtles—when they caught them. They drank rainwater—when it rained. Often there was no food and no water, and the men were hungry and thirsty. Sometimes they thought, "We are going to die soon."

Joel wrote a letter to his wife. "My dear Edith," Joel wrote. "If I die, I hope someone will send you this letter. Then you will know how I died. I had the best in life—a great woman and beautiful children. I love you, Edith. I love you."

In June it didn't rain for a long time, and the men ran out of water. They were thin and weak, and they thought, "We are going to die now." They put on their best clothes, lay down, and closed their eyes. After a while it began to rain. The men stood up and licked the water from the roof. Then all five men began to cry.

Ten days later, on June 15, a Japanese fishing boat found the men. They were 4,000 miles[1] from Costa Rica.

Nobody sent Joel's letter to his wife. He showed it to his wife himself. Joel will always keep the letter. The letter, he says, helps him remember. "On the ocean I realized that I love my wife and children very, very much. My family is everything to me. I don't want to forget that."

[1] 6,437 kilometers

2. VOCABULARY

Complete the sentences with the words below.

raw	survive	harbor	nets	ran out of

1. Joel went to the ___harbor___ in Puntarenas. There were many boats there.
2. The fishermen needed their ________________ to catch fish.
3. The men didn't want to eat ________________ turtle meat, so they built a fire to cook the meat.
4. The men didn't want to die on the ocean; they wanted to ________________.
5. The men had nothing to drink because they ________________ water.

3. COMPREHENSION

FINDING INFORMATION

What information is in the story? What information is not in the story?

There are two correct ways to complete each sentence. Circle the letters of the *two* correct answers.

1. Joel Gonzalez
- **(a.)** is a fisherman.
- **b.** has four children.
- **(c.)** lives in Puntarenas, Costa Rica.

2. After the storm,
- **a.** there was a hole in the boat.
- **b.** the boat's engine and radio didn't work.
- **c.** there was no food or fresh water on the boat.

3. To survive, the men
- **a.** ate turtle meat.
- **b.** drank rainwater.
- **c.** caught birds.

4. In June the men thought they were going to die because they
- **a.** had no more water.
- **b.** were all sick.
- **c.** were thin and weak.

5. When the Japanese fishing boat found the men,
- **a.** they were 4,000 miles from Costa Rica.
- **b.** it was five months after the storm.
- **c.** only three of the fishermen were alive.

UNDERSTANDING REASONS

Find the best way to complete each sentence. Write the letter of your answer on the line.

1. The men left Puntarenas ____

2. The men reached out of their boat ____

3. The men tore down the boat's cabin ____

4. Joel wrote his wife a letter ____

5. Joel will keep his letter ____

a. to help him remember that his family is everything to him.

b. to fish on the ocean.

c. to tell her how he died.

d. to catch turtles.

e. to make a fire with the wood.

UNDERSTANDING A SUMMARY

Imagine this: You want to tell the story "A Long Fishing Trip" to a friend. You want to tell the story quickly, in only four sentences. Which four sentences tell the story best? Check (✔) your answer.

1. ____ Joel Gonzalez is a Costa Rican fisherman. One January morning, he kissed his wife goodbye and went on a fishing trip. Joel didn't return for five months. While he was away, he wrote his wife a long letter and told her he loved her very much.

2. ____ Five Costa Rican fishermen were in a terrible storm that lasted for 22 days. After the storm, they were lost at sea for five months. To survive, they ate turtles and drank rainwater. When a Japanese fishing boat found the men, they were 4,000 miles from Costa Rica.

4. DISCUSSION

Fishing is dangerous work. Do you think it is the most dangerous work in the United States?

Read the list of dangerous jobs below. Which job is the most dangerous? In a small group, take a guess. Check (✔) your group's answer.

What is the most dangerous job in the United States?

__ fisherman

__ farmer

__ police officer

__ soldier

__ construction worker

__ truck driver

__ cashier in a small store

Tell the class which job your group chose. Were you right? (The answer is in the answer key.)

5. WRITING

Joel wrote a letter to his wife. The end of Joel's letter is missing. Complete Joel's letter on your own paper.

Dear Edith,

If I die, I hope someone will send you this letter. Then you will know how I died.

When we left the harbor, everything was fine. Then, a few hours later, there was a terrible storm. It lasted for 22 days. After the storm, we checked our boat. Our fishing nets were . . .

UNIT 20

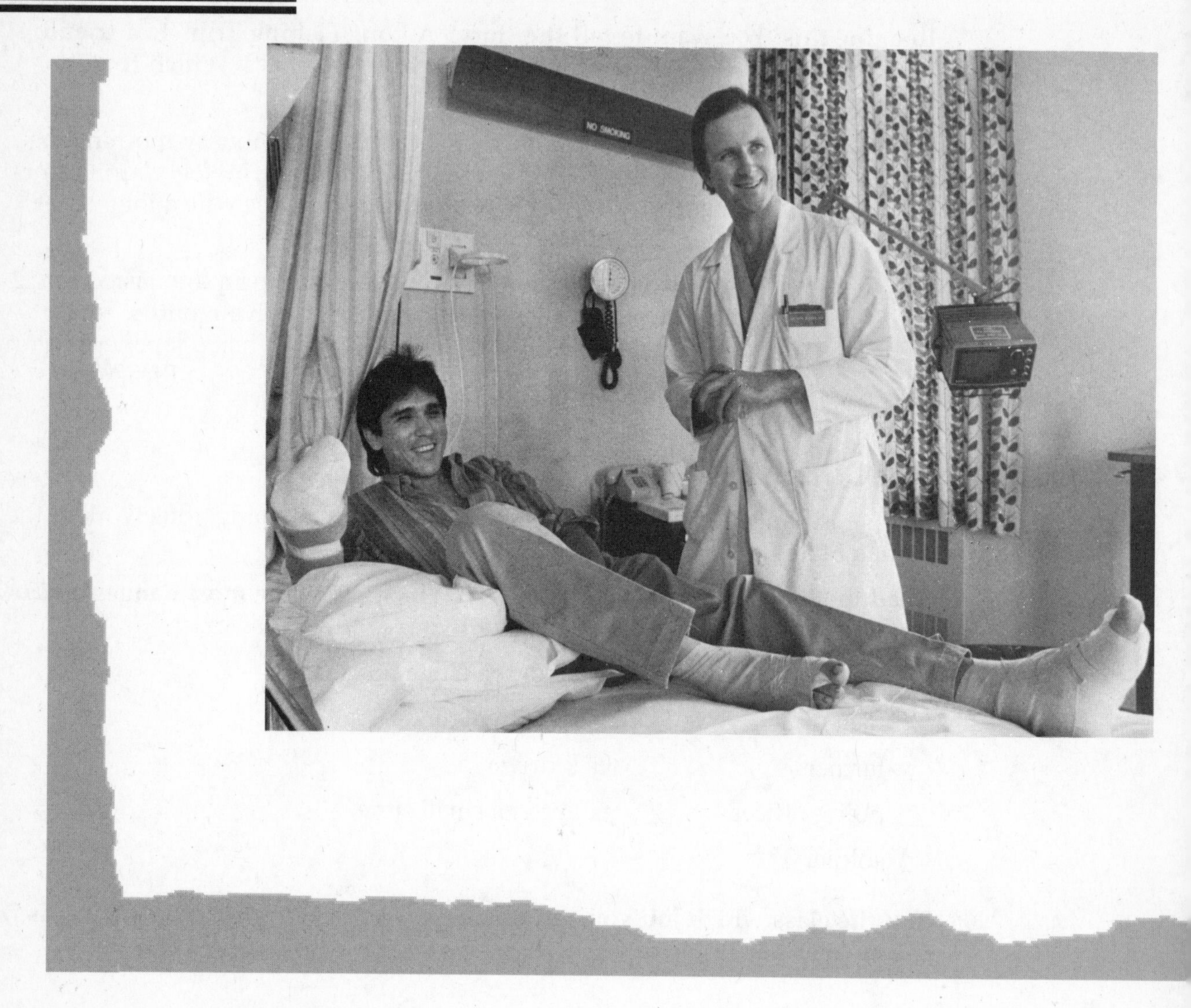

1. PRE-READING

Look at the picture.

- Where do you think the men are?
- Who is the man in the white coat?
- Look at the man on the bed. What does he have on his feet and right hand?

Read the title of the story. Look at the picture again.

- What do you think this story is about?
- Can you guess what happens?

A Surgeon Again

On September 19, 1985, Dr. Francisco Bucio was getting dressed for work. His roommate, Angel Alcantara, was combing his hair. Both Francisco and Angel were doctors in Mexico City. They lived and worked together on the fourth floor of General Hospital. Suddenly the hospital began to shake. "Earthquake!" Francisco said. The hospital shook and shook. Then the hospital collapsed. Francisco and Angel fell four floors to the ground below. Three floors of the hospital fell on top of them. The doctors were trapped under a mountain of steel and concrete.

"Angel!" Francisco called to his friend. Angel moaned in pain. Then he was silent. Francisco knew that his friend was dead.

Francisco wanted to cry because Angel was dead. But he told himself, "Keep calm." Then he realized that his right hand was hurt. "Oh no, oh no," Francisco cried. "I can't lose my right hand. My right hand is my future."

For the next four days Francisco was trapped under the hospital. Every twelve hours Angel's watch beeped exactly at 7:30. "Angel's watch helped me," Francisco said. "I knew what day it was. But I wondered about my family. Were they safe? And I wondered about Mexico City."

On the third day Francisco became very thirsty. He dreamed of rivers with no water. He dreamed of ships on dry land.

Then, on the fourth day, rescue workers found Francisco. His right hand was trapped under concrete. The rescue workers wanted to cut off Francisco's hand. Francisco's brothers said, "No!"

When rescue workers carried Francisco out of the hospital, he still had his hand. But four fingers were badly crushed. Doctors had to cut off all four fingers on Francisco's right hand. Only his thumb remained. During the next months Francisco had five operations on his hand. His hand looked better, but it didn't work well. Francisco wanted to be a surgeon. But he needed his right hand to operate on patients.

Then Francisco heard about a surgeon who was an expert in hand surgery. Six months after the earthquake, the surgeon operated on Francisco. He cut off two of Francisco's toes and sewed the toes on Francisco's hand. The toes became new fingers for Francisco, and the new fingers worked well. Francisco could operate on patients. Dr. Francisco Bucio was a surgeon again.

"Now I know how patients feel," Dr. Bucio said. "I can sympathize and understand. I had six operations, and so much pain, too much pain. Sometimes people joke. They say I'm the surgeon who operates with his feet. OK, my hand isn't beautiful, but I like it. It works."

2. VOCABULARY

Which sentence has the same meaning as the sentence in the story? Circle the letter of the correct answer.

1. The hospital *collapsed.*

a. The hospital disappeared.

b. The hospital fell down.

2. The doctors were *trapped* under a mountain of steel and concrete.

a. A mountain of steel and concrete was on top of the doctors. They couldn't move.

b. The doctors climbed a mountain of steel and concrete.

3. Angel *moaned* in pain.

a. Angel made a sound.

b. Angel closed his eyes.

4. "Now I know how patients feel," Dr. Bucio said. "I can *sympathize.*"

a. "I understand patients' feelings and pain because I, too, had a lot of pain."

b. "My patients are kind people, and I like them very much."

3. COMPREHENSION

FINDING INFORMATION

What information is in the story? What information is not in the story?

There are two correct ways to complete each sentence. Circle the letters of the *two* correct answers.

1. On September 19, 1985,
- **a.** there was an earthquake in Mexico City.
- **b.** the airport in Mexico City was damaged.
- **c.** General Hospital in Mexico City collapsed.

2. During the four days Francisco was trapped under the hospital, he
- **a.** heard the rescue workers.
- **b.** wondered about his family.
- **c.** became very thirsty.

3. When rescue workers carried Francisco out of the hospital,
- **a.** he still had both hands.
- **b.** the fingers on his right hand were badly crushed.
- **c.** his brothers cried with happiness.

4. The surgeon who was an expert in hand surgery
- **a.** cut off two of Francisco's toes.
- **b.** sewed the toes on Francisco's right hand.
- **c.** worked at General Hospital in Mexico City.

5. Today Francisco Bucio
- **a.** lives in the United States.
- **b.** is a surgeon again.
- **c.** knows how his patients feel.

UNDERSTANDING TIME RELATIONSHIPS

Find the best way to complete each sentence. Write the letter of your answer on the line.

1. On September 19, 1985, ____
2. Every twelve hours ____
3. On the third day ____
4. On the fourth day ____
5. Six months after the earthquake, ____

a. rescue workers found Francisco.
b. an expert in hand surgery operated on Francisco.
c. Francisco became very thirsty.
d. Angel's watch beeped.
e. there was an earthquake in Mexico City.

UNDERSTANDING A SUMMARY

Imagine this: You want to tell the story "A Surgeon Again" to a friend. You want to tell the story quickly, in only five sentences. Which five sentences tell the story best? Check (✔) your answer.

1. ____ A hospital in Mexico City collapsed during an earthquake. One of the doctors was trapped under the hospital for four days. He was rescued, but the fingers on his right hand were badly crushed, and doctors had to cut them off. Later, an expert in hand surgery cut off two of the doctor's toes and sewed the toes on the doctor's right hand. The doctor is now a surgeon again and can operate on patients.

2. ____ In 1985 there was an earthquake in Mexico City, and a hospital collapsed. A doctor who lived and worked in the hospital fell four floors to the ground below. Three floors of the hospital fell on top of him, and he was trapped under a mountain of steel and concrete. During his four days under the hospital, the doctor worried about his right hand. He also worried about his family and about Mexico City.

4. DISCUSSION

On September 19, 1985, there was an earthquake in Mexico. An earthquake is a natural disaster.

On the map below, look at the places where natural disasters sometimes happen in the United States. Discuss new vocabulary with your classmates.

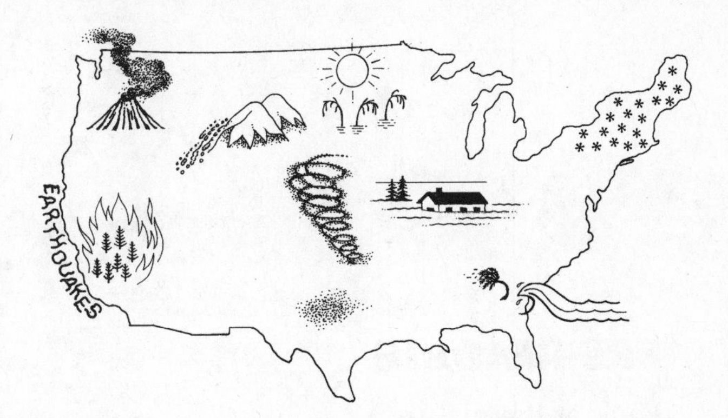

On your own paper, draw a map of your native country. Mark the places where natural disasters sometimes happen. Then show your map to a partner. Tell your partner about natural disasters in your native country.

5. WRITING

Look at the map you drew for the discussion exercise. Then, on your own paper, write about natural disasters that sometimes happen in your native country. Or, write about a natural disaster that *you* experienced.

UNIT 21

1. PRE-READING

Look at the picture.

- How old do you think the girl is?
- What pictures do you see on the balloon?

Read the title of the story. Look at the picture again.

- What do you think this story is about?
- Can you guess what happens?

The Mermaid Balloon

"Grandma!" little Desiree exclaimed. "It's my daddy's birthday. How will I send him a birthday card?"

Desiree's grandmother looked at Desiree and sighed. She didn't know what to say. Desiree's father had died nine months earlier. Desiree didn't understand. She was only four years old.

"I have an idea," her grandmother said. "Let's write your daddy a letter. We can tie the letter to a balloon and send it up to heaven. What should we write?"

Desiree told her grandmother to write, "Happy Birthday, Daddy. I love you and miss you. Please write me on my birthday in January."

Desiree's grandmother wrote Desiree's message and their address on a small piece of paper. Then Desiree, her mother, and her grandmother went to a store to buy a balloon. Desiree looked quickly at the helium-filled balloons and said, "That one! The one with the mermaid!"

They bought the mermaid balloon and tied Desiree's letter to it. Then Desiree let the balloon go.

Desiree released the balloon in California. The wind caught the balloon and carried it east. Four days later, it came down 3,000 miles away, near a lake in eastern Canada. The name of the lake was Mermaid Lake.

Wade MacKinnon, a Canadian man, was hunting ducks at Mermaid Lake when he found Desiree's balloon and letter. He took them home to his wife. She decided to send Desiree a birthday present. She also wrote her a letter. The letter said:

Dear Desiree,

Happy Birthday from your daddy. I guess you wonder who we are. Well, my husband, Wade, went duck hunting, and guess what he found? A mermaid balloon that you sent your daddy. There are no stores in heaven, so your daddy wanted someone to do his shopping for him. I think he picked us because we live in a town called Mermaid. I know your daddy loves you very much and will always watch over you.

Lots of love,
The MacKinnons

Desiree's mother wrote the MacKinnons to thank them. During the next few weeks, she and the MacKinnons telephoned each other often. Then Desiree, her mother, and her grandmother flew to Canada to meet the MacKinnons. The MacKinnons took them to Mermaid Lake and showed them where the balloon landed.

Now, whenever Desiree wants to talk about her father, she calls the MacKinnons. After she talks to them, she feels better.

People often say, "What a coincidence—the mermaid balloon landed at Mermaid Lake!" Desiree's mother is not sure it was just a coincidence. She says, "I think that somehow my husband picked the MacKinnons. It was his way to send his love to Desiree. She understands now that her father is with her always."

2. VOCABULARY

Which words have the same meaning as the words in the story? Circle the letter of your answer.

1. "Grandma!" Desiree *exclaimed.* "It's my daddy's birthday!"
   a. said suddenly, with strong feeling
   b. said slowly, with a very quiet voice

2. Desiree *released the balloon.*
   a. opened her eyes and looked at the balloon
   b. opened her hand and let the balloon go

3. Wade MacKinnon was *hunting* ducks.
   a. trying to shoot
   b. trying to paint

4. Desiree's mother thinks her husband *picked* the MacKinnons to send his love to Desiree.
   a. chose
   b. paid

3. COMPREHENSION

UNDERSTANDING THE MAIN IDEA

Circle the letter of your answer.

1. What was the coincidence in the story?
 a. Desiree and her father have the same birthday, January 12.
 b. The mermaid balloon came down at Mermaid Lake.
 c. The MacKinnons also have a four-year-old daughter.

2. Desiree feels better now because
 a. she got a lot of presents for her birthday.
 b. she can talk to the MacKinnons about her father.
 c. she spends a lot of time with her grandmother.

REMEMBERING DETAILS

One word in each sentence is not correct. Find the word and cross it out. Write the correct word.

1. Desiree tied a ~~present~~ letter to a helium-filled balloon.

2. The balloon had a picture of a fish on it.

3. Desiree released the balloon in Arizona.

4. The wind carried the balloon south.

5. Four years later, the balloon came down 3,000 miles away.

6. The balloon landed near a mountain in eastern Canada.

7. A Canadian man was feeding ducks when he found Desiree's letter.

8. The MacKinnons decided to send Desiree a birthday cake and a letter.

FINDING MORE INFORMATION

Read each sentence on the left. Which sentences on the right give you more information? Match the sentences. Write the letter of your answer on the line.

1. ____ Desiree wrote her father a *letter*.	**a.** It was in eastern Canada, and its name was Mermaid Lake.
2. ____ Desiree chose a *balloon* at the store.	**b.** It said, "Happy Birthday. I love you and miss you."
3. ____ The balloon came down near a *lake*.	**c.** It was filled with helium, and it had a picture of a mermaid on it.
4. ____ A Canadian *man* found the balloon.	**d.** His name was Wade MacKinnon, and he was hunting ducks.

4. DISCUSSION

The mermaid balloon landed at Mermaid Lake. That was a coincidence. Can you find any coincidences among your classmates?

Complete the sentences. (Skip the sentences you can't complete.)

1. My birthday is ____________________ ____________________ .
(month) (day)

2. Once I broke a bone in my ____________________ .

3. Last summer I took a trip to ____________________ .

4. A car I like is ____________________ .

5. I really need ____________________ .

6. Last night I dreamed about ____________________ .

In a small group, take turns reading your sentences. Did any students complete a sentence in the same way? Tell the class about any coincidences you discovered.

5. WRITING

Write a letter. Put your letter in a small plastic bag. Tie the plastic bag to a helium-filled balloon and let the balloon go.

Here is the letter that one student wrote.

My name is Andrea. I am a student at the American Language Institute in Indiana, PA. If you find my letter, please write me and tell me how far my balloon went.
My address is:

American Language Institute
Eicher Hall
Indiana University of Pennsylvania
Indiana, PA 15705

One more thing: I am from Slovakia, but I speak English.

Now write your letter on your own paper.

UNIT 22

1. PRE-READING

Look at the picture.

- How old do you think the woman is?
- Who do you think the child is?
- Can you guess when the woman lived?

Read the title of the story. Look at the picture again.

- What do you think this story is about?
- Can you guess what happens?

The Two Lives of Mary Sutton

Do you believe in reincarnation—that you lived before? Jenny Cockell does. Jenny is a 40-year-old English woman. She is a doctor, and she lives with her husband and two children. That is Jenny's present life. Jenny believes she also had a past life. She believes she was Mary Sutton, an Irish woman who died in 1932.

When Jenny was four years old, she began dreaming about a woman named Mary. She had the same dreams again and again. In one dream, the woman was standing on a beach and looking at the ocean. She seemed to be waiting for someone. In one terrible dream, the woman was lying in bed in a white room. She was dying.

Sometimes in her dreams Jenny saw the woman's village. Jenny thought that it was on the coast of Ireland. Often she looked at a map of Ireland and read the names of villages on the coast. One name—Malahide—seemed familiar. Jenny thought that maybe Malahide was the woman's village.

Jenny dreamed about Mary and Mary's village all her life. Finally, when she was 36 years old, she decided to travel to Ireland.

When Jenny arrived in Malahide, she knew immediately that it was the village in her dreams. The streets, the shops, and the churches all looked familiar. She was in Mary's village!

Jenny decided to look for Mary's little house. She had seen it often in her dreams. It was on a narrow road south of the village. Jenny walked to the south end of the village and found a narrow road. She walked down the road, but there was no house. There was only an old barn.

When Jenny got back to England, she wrote a letter to the man who owned the barn. "Was there ever a small house near your barn?" she asked him.

"Yes," the man wrote back. "There was once a small house near the barn. A family with six children lived there. The mother died in childbirth in 1932. Her name was Mary Sutton."

Jenny found out that after Mary died, Mary's husband couldn't take care of their children. He gave them to other people, and they grew up apart. Jenny decided to find Mary's children. Two of the six children had died, but Jenny found the four surviving children. "Please meet me in Malahide," Jenny wrote them.

In Malahide, Mary's children, who are now in their sixties and seventies, told Jenny stories about their childhood.

Sonny, the oldest child, said, "When I was twelve I got a job on an island near Malahide. Every evening a boat brought me home. My mother often waited for me on the beach."

After talking to the Sutton children, Jenny is sure that she is the reincarnation of their mother. Some of the Sutton children think so, too. Sonny Sutton, who is 35 years older than Jenny, says, "To me, she is my mother."

2. VOCABULARY

Complete the sentences with the words below.

surviving	barn	village	childhood

1. Only a few hundred people live in Malahide. It is a ___village___ .
2. Jenny walked down a narrow road south of the village, but she saw no house. She saw only a building where animals sleep. She saw a ________________ .
3. Two of Mary's six children had died, but Jenny found the four children who were alive. She found the ________________ children.
4. The Sutton children told Jenny about the time when they were children in Malahide. They told stories about their ________________ .

3. COMPREHENSION

UNDERSTANDING THE MAIN IDEA

Circle the letter of the best answer.

1. Jenny believes she is the reincarnation of Mary Sutton because

a. Mary Sutton was her grandmother.

b. she saw Mary's life in her dreams.

c. most people in England believe in reincarnation.

2. Jenny's dreams gave her a lot of information about Mary's life. All of the information was

a. wonderful.

b. sad.

c. correct.

FINDING MORE INFORMATION

Read each sentence on the left. Which sentence on the right gives you more information? Match the sentences. Write the letter of your answer on the line.

1. ____ Jenny Cockell has a *present life.*

2. ____ Jenny believes she also had a *past life.*

3. ____ In her dreams Jenny saw the woman's *village.*

4. ____ Jenny looked for *Mary's house.*

5. ____ Jenny looked for *Mary's children.*

a. It was on the coast of Ireland, and its name was Malahide.

b. She believes she was Mary Sutton, an Irish woman who died in 1932.

c. It was on a narrow road south of the village.

d. She lives in England with her husband and two children.

e. They are in their sixties and seventies now.

REMEMBERING DETAILS

Read each sentence. If the sentence describes Jenny Cockell, write a *J* for Jenny. If the sentence describes Mary Sutton, write an *M* for Mary.

1. __J__ She lives in England.

2. __M__ She lived in Ireland.

3. ____ She had six children.

4. ____ She often looked at maps of Ireland.

5. ____ She is 40 years old.

6. ____ Her son worked on an island

7. ____ She dreamed about a womar

8. ____ She lived in a little house on narrow road.

4. DISCUSSION

When she was a child, Jenny drew a map of the village she saw in her dreams. Look at the map that Jenny drew. Then look at an actual map of Malahide, Ireland.

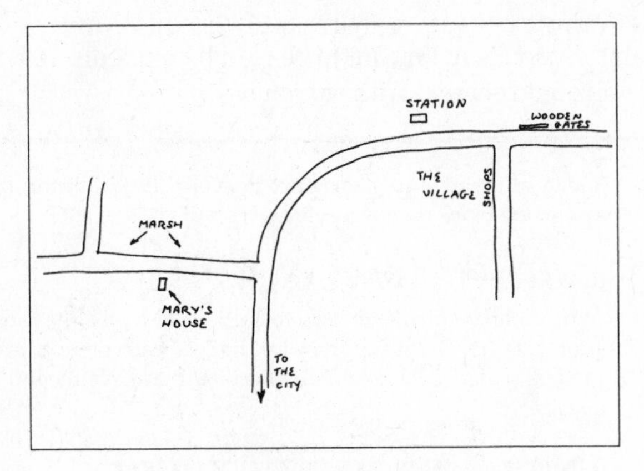

Jenny's Map

Actual Map of Malahide, Ireland

Think about the story and the two maps. Then read the questions and check (✔) your answers. Explain your answers in a small group.

1. Do you believe that Jenny Cockell is the reincarnation of Mary Sutton?

__ Yes

__ No

__ Maybe

2. Do you believe that you have a past life—that you lived before?

__ Yes

__ No

__ Maybe

5. WRITING

When Jenny was in Malahide, she kept a diary. She wrote down everything she saw and did.

Complete Jenny's diary on your own paper.

June 3

When I arrived in Malahide, I went to a small hotel in the center of the village. After I unpacked my suitcase, I ate lunch at the hotel. Then I went outside to look around the village . . .

To the Teacher

The original newspaper and magazine versions of MORE TRUE STORIES contain information that could not be included in the adaptations. Sometimes the information was too complicated to include; sometimes including it would have made the stories too long for the allotted space. On the other hand, the information—in many cases, the story behind the story—was just too interesting to leave out entirely. So, it was decided that additional facts would be given here, in a special "To the Teacher" section.

As you will see from the sophistication of the language, this section is not meant to be read by students. If, however, you think the information adds interest or clarity to a story, you could share it with students.

UNIT 1—PUPPY LOVE

An Okinawa newspaper, the *Ryuku Shimpo,* reported that Marilyn and Shiro became the parents of six puppies. Marilyn's owners received requests for a puppy from people all over Japan.

Shiro's pedigree is described as "mutt." The Nakamuras found him in the garbage when he was a puppy.

UNIT 2—SURPRISE! IT'S YOUR WEDDING!

After the wedding, John said of Lynn, "She's great fun to be with and often does practical jokes, but I didn't think she'd dare do anything like this."

It is not known if Lynn and John lived happily ever after.

UNIT 3—THE TRAIN

The *Hartford Courant* likened Nicole's experience to a "scene from a nail-biter movie."

There were 12 inches of clearance between the railroad ties and the underside of the train. Something scraped Nicole's thigh and a piece of gravel thrown up by the wheels struck her right temple, but those were her only injuries.

UNIT 4—THE GIFT

Felipe died after a blood vessel burst in his head. Doctors called his heart "a perfect match" for Donna. After the transplant, Donna lived a fairly normal life for three years. Then Felipe's heart began to fail her, and she was put on the waiting list for another heart transplant. Before a second donor was found, however, Donna died of heart failure while taking a nap at home. She was 17 years old.

UNIT 5—OH BOY, WHAT A RIDE!

Rocco drove the family station wagon on a four-lane road through several major intersections and past exit lanes that led to a highway.

His punishment was loss of TV and VCR privileges, although it was unlikely he would miss watching TV. He was too busy giving interviews and appearing on *Late Night with David Letterman.*

UNIT 6—THE TWINS OF SIAM

Chang and Eng first asked to be separated before their marriages. Doctors said the operation would be dangerous but agreed to try it. The story goes that just as the operation was about to begin, Sarah and Adelaide rushed in to say they loved the twins too much to let them risk their lives. They said they would marry the twins the way they were.

The term "Siamese twins" originates with Chang and Eng. The preferred term today is "conjoined twins." The phenomenon occurs when a single fertilized egg fails to completely separate into identical twins. It happens once in every 100,000 births, but many conjoined twins do not survive.

UNIT 7—THE BABY EXCHANGE

When Selma brought her baby to the Souza's house, the two mothers didn't say a word at first; they just hugged each other and sobbed.

Both couples later sued the hospital that gave them the wrong babies.

UNIT 8—WHY CAN'T THEY QUIT?

Students might be curious to know which country has the biggest smoking habit. According to a World Health Organization study cited in the *New York Times,* it is China, where 61% of the men smoke. Other countries where smoking is popular are Japan, where 60% of the men smoke; France (48%); India (40%); Britain (31%); and the United States (28%). These statistics are for males only. The country with the highest percentage of female smokers is France, where 32% of adult women smoke.

UNIT 9— EVERYBODY'S BABY

The well was 120 feet deep. Jessica went down only 20 feet because it was at that depth that the well narrowed to six inches across.

During the last hours of Jessica's 58-hour ordeal, many of the 25 men who were taking turns drilling cried every time they heard Jessica cry.

In the photo, Jessica is holding a clump of hair in her left hand. That is her own hair, which she pulled out during her days in the well.

UNIT 10—PLEASE PASS THE BIRD BRAINS

In the first edition of *More True Stories,* "Queen's Secret," one meal at the restaurant, was described as containing meat from a chicken with black feathers. Several teachers wrote to say that their Chinese students insisted the ingredient was chicken with black *skin,* not black feathers, so the description was changed.

The "dinosaur bones" in Lover's Soup are actually the ground fossils of dinosaur bones. They sell for about seven dollars a pound.

UNIT 11—MARGARET PATRICK . . . MEET RUTH EISENBERG

The two pianists call themselves Ebony and Ivory. Mrs. Eisenberg told the *North Jersey Suburbanite,* "We were great before, but now we are smashing."

UNIT 12—THE BED

Honda sponsors its Idea Contest in the hope that a marketable idea or two may emerge. Consequently, most of the entries are prototypes for new vehicles. Hiroyuki's entry was an exception.

UNIT 13—DEAR MR. ANDROPOV

After her return to the United States, Samantha appeared on the *Tonight Show* and caught the eye of Robert Wagner, who was looking for a girl to play the part of his daughter on a new TV series. Samantha read for the part and got it. The first four episodes of the series were filmed in England. Samantha and her father were returning from England when the twin-engine plane transporting them to their hometown in Maine crashed. None of the eight people aboard survived. The TV series was abandoned; the show's producer told *People* magazine that in just four episodes "Samantha's personality was so ingrained, she's irreplaceable."

UNIT 14—PARENTS AT SCHOOL

The "parents at school" program is now used in at least 700 schools in the United States. When the program was introduced at a school in Pittsburg, California, 50 students had to bring a parent to class. Of the 50 students, 48 never got into trouble again.

UNIT 15—FINDERS KEEPERS?

At first, the Columbus police department hoped the 10 percent reward would prompt people to turn in money voluntarily. However, as time went on, and only a few more people came forward with money, the police department decided to get tough. The police announced that people who kept money would be charged with a felony. One police officer told the *Columbus Dispatch,* "A lot of people think it's finders-keepers, like when they were a kid, but this is theft." The police admitted that while filing charges would be easy, the odds of getting convictions were remote.

Months after the truck spilled its cargo, people were still searching along the highway, hoping to find a few stray bills.

UNIT 16—THE AUCTION

Katie's parents had health insurance, but they were not sure it would cover all of Katie's medical bills.

Katie told the *Columbus Dispatch* that while her lamb was being auctioned, "I stared hard at my dad's face. I was crying. It was great, and it seemed like forever. I didn't know how many times it sold." Katie's mother said, " The first sale is the only one that I remember, because after that I was crying too hard."

Katie's cancer is in remission, and her doctor is hopeful that it will not recur.

UNIT 17—MONEY TO BURN

Lillian intended to dry the money for only 40 seconds in her microwave oven, but by force of habit set the timer for five minutes—the time she routinely baked a potato.

The farmer in the story sent the cow's stomach to the Treasury Department because he had been advised to sent the money in the container it was destroyed in.

The U.S. Treasury Department will reimburse people the full amount of any damaged bill if their experts can put at least 51 percent of the bill together.

UNIT 18—A CHANCE TO LIVE AGAIN

Dr. Paul Segall, the Trans Time scientist who froze a dog in 1987, was so confident that the experiment would be successful, he chose as his subject his family's beloved beagle, Miles. The beagle recovered fully from being frozen and became a celebrity, appearing on several talk shows.

Some people have elected to have Trans Time freeze only their brains after their deaths, hoping that future scientists will be able to clone them so that they are essentially the same person, with their knowledge and memories intact.

UNIT 19—A LONG FISHING TRIP

The fishermen's five-month ordeal set a world record for survival at sea; the previous record was held by a Chinese sailor who drifted alone in the Atlantic for 133 days during World War II.

In the discussion exercise, students guess which job is the most dangerous. The information on dangerous work comes from the *Occupational Outlook Quarterly,* which compiles statistics on the number of fatal injuries in a particular line of work compared to the percent of the labor force doing that work in a given year. Truck driving ranks as the most dangerous work because truck drivers suffer 12 percent of all fatal injuries but make up only 2 percent of the work force. Construction workers and cashiers each account for 9 percent of all fatalities, but construction work is statistically more dangerous because construction workers make up only 4 percent of the work force, cashiers 12 percent.

UNIT 20—A SURGEON AGAIN

The San Francisco surgeon who operated on Francisco was assisted by a team of eight surgeons. In a 14-hour operation, they took one toe from each of Francisco's feet and attached them to his hand as the ring and pinkie fingers.

Today Dr. Bucio is in private practice in Tijuana, Mexico. He is a plastic surgeon.

UNIT 21—THE MERMAID BALLOON

The MacKinnons, who are themselves the parents of three young daughters, debated for weeks about the best way to reply to Desiree's letter. The letter in the story is the actual letter, slightly abridged to save space, that Mrs. MacKinnon wrote to Desiree.

The story of the mermaid balloon is told in a made-for-TV movie filmed by Atlantis, a Canadian company.

UNIT 22—THE TWO LIVES OF MARY SUTTON

When Mary's surviving children met with Jenny, they were astonished to hear her describe in great detail their childhood cottage, which had been torn down in 1959. She also described a scene she had seen while under hypnosis. She said that the children were upset because they had caught a rabbit in a trap and the rabbit was still alive. Sonny remembered the incident. In her book *Across Time and Death,* Jenny writes: "This information really shocked him by its accuracy. The incident was so private to him and his family, how could anyone else know about it?"

Under hypnosis, Jenny has seen scenes of yet another previous life, of a French girl who lived in the 1700s, and scenes from a future life, of a Nepalese girl who will be born in the next century.

Some students who participated in the initial field-testing of this story voiced strong opinions about reincarnation. It might be a good idea to remind students in multicultural classes that the concept of reincarnation is not widely accepted in the West and Middle East but is a commonly held belief in Asia. It is hoped that the discussion exercise prompts students to express their opinions, but in a way that is sensitive to classmates who have different religious beliefs.

ANSWER KEY

UNIT 1

Vocabulary
1. missing **2.** shivering **3.** curious **4.** amazed **5.** famous

Understanding the Main Idea
1. c **2.** b

Understanding Cause and Effect
1. c **2.** d **3.** b **4.** a **5.** e

Reviewing the Story
1. disappeared **2.** came **3.** was **4.** followed **5.** swim **6.** girlfriend **7.** about **8.** distance **9.** rough **10.** famous **11.** love

UNIT 2

Vocabulary
1. patient **2.** trick **3.** courthouse **4.** wedding **5.** punch

Understanding the Main Idea
1. c **2.** b

Understanding Connections
1. b **2.** d **3.** a **4.** c

Remembering Details
1. ~~angry~~/afraid **2.** ~~brothers~~/parents **3.** ~~party~~/wedding
4. ~~boss~~/friend **5.** ~~Monday~~/Saturday **6.** ~~problem~~/trick
7. ~~library~~/courthouse **8.** ~~telephoned~~/saw **9.** ~~Bob's~~/John's
10. ~~boyfriend~~/husband

UNIT 3

Vocabulary
1. a **2.** b **3.** a. **4.** b

Remembering Details
1. ~~winter~~/spring **2.** ~~four~~/eight **3.** ~~rocks~~/fish **4.** ~~quiet~~/loud
5. ~~truck~~/train **6.** ~~walked~~/ran **7.** ~~sitting~~/lying **8.** ~~hours~~/seconds
9. ~~top~~/bottom **10.** ~~Dad~~/Mom

Understanding Cause and Effect
1. c **2.** a **3.** d **4.** b

Understanding a Summary
1

UNIT 4

Vocabulary
1. kidding **2.** sharp **3.** dizzy **4.** rushed **5.** checkup

Understanding the Main Idea
1. b **2.** c

Understanding Pronouns
1. e **2.** a **3.** b **4.** d **5.** f **6.** c

Finding More Information
1. d **2.** a **3.** c **4.** b

UNIT 5

Vocabulary
1. coffee break **2.** station wagon **3.** rush hour **4.** heavy **5.** siren

Understanding the Main Idea
1. b **2.** b

Understanding Reasons
1. d **2.** a **3.** c **4.** e **5.** b

Remembering Details
1. ~~salesman~~/police officer **2.** ~~evening~~/morning **3.** ~~woman~~/man
4. ~~fixing~~/driving **5.** ~~hit~~/followed **6.** ~~50~~/5 **7.** ~~television~~/refrigerator
8. ~~seat~~/door **9.** ~~light~~/heavy **10.** ~~mechanics~~/reporters

UNIT 6

Vocabulary
1. a **2.** a **3.** b **4.** b

Understanding the Main Idea
1. c **2.** b

Remembering Details
1. ~~China~~/Thailand **2.** ~~doctors~~/twins **3.** ~~laugh~~/stare
4. ~~Australian~~/American **5.** ~~days~~/years **6.** ~~cousins~~/sisters
7. ~~unhappy~~/happy **8.** ~~can~~/can't

Understanding Reasons
1. d **2.** c **3.** a **4.** b

UNIT 7

Vocabulary
1. a **2.** b **3.** a **4.** a

Understanding the Main Idea
1. b **2.** c

Understanding Cause and Effect
1. e. **2.** c **3.** d **4.** a **5.** b

Understanding a Summary
1

UNIT 8

Vocabulary
1. quit **2.** pack **3.** causes **4.** get used to

Understanding the Main Idea
1. c **2.** b

Finding More Information
1. c **2.** d **3.** a **4.** b

Reviewing the Story
1. addicted **2.** drug **3.** smoking **4.** weight **5.** gum **6.** little **7.** chew **8.** quit **9.** smoke **10.** way

UNIT 9

Vocabulary
1. day care center **2.** narrow **3.** dialed **4.** drill **5.** injured

Understanding the Main Idea
1. b **2.** c

Understanding Time Relationships
1. d **2.** c **3.** e **4.** a **5.** b

Remembering Details
1. ~~years~~/months **2.** ~~kitchen~~/yard **3.** ~~water~~/well **4.** ~~wrote~~/dialed
5. ~~cover~~/hole **6.** ~~soft~~/solid **7.** ~~down~~/up **8.** ~~doctors~~/paramedics
9. ~~old~~/young **10.** ~~rock~~/cover

UNIT 10

Vocabulary
1. ground **2.** centuries **3.** common **4.** digestion

Understanding the Main Idea
1. b **2.** a

Remembering Details
1. ~~furniture~~/food **2.** ~~backaches~~/headaches **3.** ~~beef~~/pearls
4. ~~red~~/gray **5.** ~~delicious~~/medicinal **6.** ~~months~~/centuries
7. ~~short~~/long **8.** ~~bakery~~/restaurant

Finding More Information
1. d **2.** b **3.** c **4.** a

UNIT 11

Vocabulary
1. a **2.** b **3.** b **4.** b

Understanding Connections
1. b **2.** d **3.** a **4.** e **5.** c

Making Inferences
1. b **2.** d **3.** a **4.** c

Understanding a Summary
2

UNIT 12

Vocabulary
1. a **2.** a **3.** b. **4.** b

Finding Information
1. He made a special bed.
2. It is for people who oversleep.
3. It is connected to an alarm clock.
4. It has a tape recorder.
5. He works for Honda Motor Company.
6. He made the bed because he wanted to win a contest.

Remembering Details
An alarm clock will ring.
A tape recorder will play a recording of his girlfriend.
The tape recorder will play a recording of his boss.
A mechanical foot will kick Hiroyuki in the head.
The bed will rise higher and higher.
Hiroyuki will slide onto the floor.

Understanding Cause and Effect
1. c **2.** a **3.** b **4.** d

UNIT 13

Vocabulary
1. enemies **2.** frightened **3.** cheerful **4.** astronomer

Finding Information
1. a, c **2.** a, b **3.** b, c **4.** a, b **5.** a, c **6.** a, b

Understanding Reasons
1. e **2.** d **3.** b **4.** c **5.** a

Reviewing the Story
1. letter **2.** about **3.** war **4.** visit **5.** Soviet **6.** girl **7.** countries
8. book **9.** children **10.** peace

UNIT 14

Vocabulary
1. b **2.** c **3.** b **4.** c

Understanding the Main Idea
1. b **2.** c

Understanding Cause and Effect
1. c **2.** a **3.** e **4.** b **5.** d

Understanding a Summary
1

UNIT 15

Vocabulary
1. armored truck **2.** ripped **3.** slammed on their brakes
4. grabbing

Remembering Details
1. ~~quiet~~/busy **2.** ~~bus~~/truck **3.** ~~closed~~/opened **4.** ~~paper~~/plastic
5. ~~leaves~~/money **6.** ~~houses~~/cars **7.** ~~thirty~~/twenty **8.** ~~tax~~/reward
9. ~~pennies~~/dollars

Understanding Time Relationships
1. c **2.** b **3.** a **4.** e **5.** d

Making Inferences
1. b **2.** a **3.** e. **4.** d **5.** c

UNIT 16

Vocabulary
1. crowd **2.** auctioneer **3.** chanted **4.** cheered

Remembering Details
1. ~~cow~~/lamb **2.** ~~Seven~~/Seventeen **3.** ~~December~~/July
4. ~~world~~/county **5.** ~~lowest~~/highest **6.** ~~cents~~/dollars
7. ~~auctioneer~~/farmer **8.** ~~thanked~~/paid

Understanding Cause and Effect
1. e **2.** d **3.** a **4.** b **5.** c

Understanding a Summary
2

UNIT 17

Vocabulary
1. income **2.** refund **3.** set the timer **4.** experts

Remembering Details
She put it in her pocket./She washed it with her jeans./She put it on the kitchen table to dry./She burned it in her microwave oven./She showed it to a teller at the bank./She sent it to the Treasury Department./She gave it to friends.

Understanding Pronouns
1. b **2.** c **3.** h **4.** d **5.** e **6.** f **7.** a **8.** g

Understanding a Summary
2

UNIT 18

Vocabulary
1. b **2.** a **3.** b **4.** a

Understanding the Main Idea
1. b **2.** a

Finding Information
1. b, c **2.** a, c **3.** b, c **4.** a, b **5.** a, b

Making Inferences
1. b **2.** a **3.** c **4.** d

UNIT 19

Vocabulary
1. harbor **2.** nets **3.** raw **4.** survive **5.** ran out of

Finding Information
1. a, c **2.** b, c **3.** a, b **4.** a, c **5.** a, b

Understanding Reasons
1. b **2.** d **3.** e **4.** c **5.** a

Understanding a Summary
2

Discussion
The most dangerous jobs, in order, are:
1. truck driver (because of accidents)
2. construction worker
3. cashier in a small store (because of robberies)
4. farmer
5. police officer
6. soldier
7. fisherman

UNIT 20

Vocabulary
1. b **2.** a **3.** a **4.** a

Finding Information
1. a, c **2.** b, c **3.** a, b **4.** a, b **5.** b, c

Understanding Time Relationships
1. e **2.** d **3.** c **4.** a **5.** b

Understanding a Summary
1

UNIT 21

Vocabulary
1. a **2.** b **3.** a **4.** a

Understanding the Main Idea
1. b **2.** b

Remembering Details
1. ~~present~~/letter **2.** ~~fish~~/mermaid **3.** ~~Arizona~~/California
4. ~~south~~/east **5.** ~~years~~/days **6.** ~~mountain~~/lake
7. ~~feeding~~/hunting **8.** ~~cake~~/present

Finding More Information
1. b **2.** c **3.** a **4.** d

UNIT 22

Vocabulary
1. village **2.** barn **3.** surviving **4.** childhood

Understanding the Main Idea
1. b **2.** c

Finding More Information
1. d **2.** b **3.** a **4.** c **5.** e

Remembering Details
1. J **2.** M **3.** M **4.** J **5.** J **6.** M **7.** J **8.** M